D1324427

Fully Automated
Luxury Communism

Fully Automated Luxury Communism

A Manifesto

Aaron Bastani

VERSO
London • New York

First published by Verso 2019
© Aaron Bastani 2019

The moral rights of the author have been asserted

1 3 5 7 9 10 8 6 4 2

Verso
UK: 6 Meard Street, London W1F 0EG
US: 20 Jay Street, Suite 1010, Brooklyn, NY 11201
versobooks.com

Verso is the imprint of New Left Books

ISBN-13: 978-1-78663-262-3
ISBN-13:978-1-78873-246-8 (EXPORT)
ISBN-13: 978-1-78663-265-4 (US EBK)
ISBN-13: 978-1-78663-264-7 (UK EBK)

British Library Cataloguing in Publication Data
A catalogue record for this book is available from the British Library

Library of Congress Cataloging-in-Publication Data
A catalog record for this book is available from the Library of Congress

Typeset in Fournier by MJ & N Gavan, Truro, Cornwall
Printed and bound by CPI Group (UK) Ltd, Croydon CR0 4YY

To Charlotte. This would have been
impossible without you.

Man is a living creature of varied, multiform and ever-changing nature.
Giovanni Pico della Mirandola

In bad times, I did not abandon the city; in good times, I had no private interests; in desperate times, I feared nothing.
Cardinal De Retz

Contents

Acknowledgements

Special thanks are due to Leo Hollis, my editor at Verso. A congenial yet critical voice, you have made this an infinitely better book than it otherwise would have been. Thanks also to the rest of the Verso team who have assisted in making *FALC* a reality, at least in print. Your work is invaluable in taking radical ideas to as broad an audience as possible. Long may it continue.

I would like to extend my appreciation to the whole team at Novara Media. We started a strange journey five years ago, which has taken an interesting turn. I am particularly indebted to James Butler and Ash Sarkar, whose initial scepticism has made the arguments which follow far more robust.

Thanks also to Andrew Chadwick for giving me the space to find my own voice while writing my doctorate. Above all else you demonstrated the importance of terse prose and clear argument – two things I lacked prior to our working together.

Finally, I am indebted to the many people who fought for a political settlement which gave me free healthcare and cheap education. Without you I would not be alive, let alone writing a book. There is no greater source of inspiration for the struggles that lie ahead than your accomplishments, which, although in the past, abide in the present.

Introduction
Six Characters in Search of a Future

Life is full of strange absurdities, which, strangely enough, do not even need to appear plausible, since they are true.

Luigi Pirandello

Yang

Yang is a factory worker in Zhengzhou, a city in the Chinese province of Henan. Born in a village in western China, her working life has corresponded with her country becoming the workshop of the world. She arrived in the city a decade ago, and since then has created a decent life for herself. While her job is exhausting – shifts often run from eleven to thirteen hours a day – Yang considers herself lucky. She is financially independent and earns enough to send money home to her parents.

Like many of her friends and co-workers, Yang is an only child. This means that while she feels fortunate on the factory floor, she is increasingly worried about the health of her ageing parents – the care of whom will soon be her responsibility.

Between that and the transience of city life, Yang views her own chances of starting a family as remote. Her duties lie elsewhere and, eventually, she will have to return home.

But alongside that hopefully distant prospect, another anxiety has recently troubled her. It was something unthinkable when she received her first pay packet as a teenager fresh from the provinces all those years ago. Work is drying up.

While Yang's earnings have been rising every year since she arrived in the city, something few people her age in Europe or North America can say, the foreman continually makes jokes about robots taking her job. Although Yang usually ignores him, the illicit trade unionists in her workplace say similar things. According to them, wages are no longer competitive because foreigners overseas have become accustomed to earning less than before. While the trade unionists see little chance of China losing its industrial eminence, that inevitably means some jobs will go abroad while others are automated. Of course many jobs will stay in China – there will always be work – but conditions won't stay as they are. Yang even read on the internet how the company she works for, Foxconn, has started to build factories in America.

Chris

When President Obama ratified the SPACE Act in 2015 it was a historic moment, at least for Chris Blumenthal. That legislation, while attracting little coverage in the press, recognised the right of private companies to make profits in space. American capitalism had a new frontier.

Today marks the anniversary of that event, and Blumenthal couldn't be happier. Alone in his condo, he watches a Falcon Heavy booster rocket alight somewhere in the mid-Atlantic. Its successful landing not only makes a manned mission to

Mars highly likely, but also continues an unblemished three-year safety record for SpaceX, the company which built it. The private space industry, for so long reliant on government contracts and the deep pockets of a few industrialists, is no longer science fiction. Soon rockets, just like this one, will be as familiar as a Boeing 737.

After watching the landing streamed on Twitter, Blumenthal – an early stage investor in an asteroid mining company – shares it with a WhatsApp group of like-minded individuals. Among them are a highly paid NBA coach and a Hollywood director. To the link Blumenthal adds – only half-ironically – 'SHOW ME THE MONEY'.

A response pops up straight away. Blumenthal doesn't know the person intimately but presumes they watched the same stream, 'There ain't enough $ in the world where this is going.' Blumenthal doesn't know it, but every other member of the group will watch the landing just like he did, although not all in real time. Some will be at home, others eating dinner with clients, friends and family. One will be lying in bed with her lover. Wherever they are, all of them will watch history unfold on the same OLED display in the palm of their hand. The technological trend allowing them to do so, ever-cheaper cameras with constantly improving resolution, ensured the rocket's pilotless landing was entirely automated.

As Blumenthal goes to check the basketball scores, Sandra – an old friend and Manhattan lawyer – chimes in: 'Our problem is there is too much of the stuff, it's going to be so easy everyone will be putting a rocket up their ass to get there next.'

Nobody responds, although the others are all aware that a sudden oversupply of minerals will mean plummeting prices. For now, that doesn't matter, and it won't for another decade at least. That's because this small group of people will be at the front of the queue when asteroid mining becomes the fastest-growing industry in history. It won't last, of course, but not much does these days.

Leia

Leia keys in the code and opens the door to start her morning shift. She walks straight over to the sound system, plugging the audio jack into her phone and presses the Spotify icon. She chooses the 'Discover Weekly' playlist – a series of songs curated by a predictive algorithm – before switching on the bar's various gadgets: glass washer, coffee machine, lights, air conditioning.

Even though the sun has only been visible in the sky for a few hours, the energy needs of the building – from its WiFi router to the CCTV on the bar and the kitchen's fridges – are met by solar power. Some is generated by photovoltaic panels fixed on the bar's roof, but most comes from a thirteen-megawatt solar farm several miles away. On the Hawaiian island of Kaua'i, where Leia was born, this is how electricity is generated.

As she begins to wipe down tables, the second track on the playlist fades out. Leia's sister, Kai – presently studying in California – is messaging her.

In what has become a customary feature of Leia's weekend shifts, Kai sends pictures of herself partying to the Facebook group they both share with innumerable family members across multiple time zones. At the foot of the picture, taken on the US–Mexico border a few moments earlier, are the words 'I miss you.'

Meanwhile, the solar farm – with its 55,000 silicon panels, three technicians and two security guards – is, like Leia, beginning its day's work. Solar City, which built and now leases the site to the island's energy cooperative, are confident that the maintenance of similar projects will soon be entirely automated. Leia doesn't know it yet, but a similar fate awaits her father, a software developer, a decade from now.

Instant global communication, just like the local transition from fossil fuels, has gone unnoticed by the teenager. For her both are simply mundane features of a world that is taken for granted. The slow elimination of her father's profession will feel no different.

Peter

Addressing a large industry event in San Antonio, Peter is in ebullient mood. Sixty this year, he has the energy of a much younger man – primarily as a result of regular injections of human growth hormone. These days he takes great pride in two things: the baseball team he owns and making ever more bullish statements about the future of technology.

His expertise and legitimacy in the field comes from having founded a company acquired by one of the digital giants at the turn of the century, and today he is delivering a speech as a favour for a friend. He quickly shifts the conversation to his preferred topic: artificial intelligence and the future of jobs:

'The first two trillion-dollar company will be Amazon, no question. Bezos won't be the first trillionaire, but he'll do fine. Who comes after? SpaceX? I don't think so, we've had that technology for seventy years, and soon everyone will be doing it – but good luck to Elon. No, the first trillionaire will come from creating AI. Imagine … it is going to be as if you were doing accountancy in Victorian England and suddenly a rival has a laptop with a quad-core processor – they wipe you out. And jobs? Once that technology is rolled out most people – and this doesn't make me happy to say it – will be superfluous ... unnecessary.'

Peter shares the stage with Anya, a younger CEO from Sweden: 'Can I say, Peter, that I agree – AI changes a lot,' Anya adds. 'It challenges how we understand value, work, and even capitalism. In fact I imagine that in the future, lower classes of citizen won't have inferior or less market-able skills, they'll just lack access to personal AI. How do you have a fair labour market when that happens? I don't think you can.'

'I'm telling you', Peter butts in, his tone almost oblivious to the large audience, 'the first asshole who builds an AI is a trillionaire.' He relaxes back into his chair before wistfully adding what sounds like an internal monologue, 'He is either a trillionaire or a jackass.'

Federica

Federica knew she had forgotten an errand – she'd promised her nephew a football jersey for his birthday but didn't order it. Now she was doing something she didn't miss: buying a gift on Oxford Circus in London's West End.

As she walks into the store Federica swipes her hand in front of her face. The gesture activates a retinal display and summons her digital personal assistant, Alex, whose voice replaces her favourite podcast in her Bluetooth earpiece. 'Hello Fede. What can I help you with?'

'Hey Alex', she responds. 'Where can I find an Arsenal shirt for Tom in here?'

Alex, a moderately powerful artificial intelligence developed by one of the major tech giants, answers almost immediately. 'Tom's size is in stock, so you won't need to wait while it's printed. First floor, on the right towards the back – I'll show you.' A map flashes in front of Federica's left eye, not that she can tell which one it is anymore. Alex continues, 'Tom has talked several times about preferring the black and gold away strip. Shall we get it?'

'Great, yes Alex, you're a lifesaver.' Looking at the lines of adult men's tracksuits, Federica remembers something. 'Alex, how is George's diet going?' George is her partner.

'Not so well,' Alex responds, 'but I think he'd rather that was discussed between the two of you.' Federica couldn't help but smile. Digital personal assistants hadn't always been so 'emotionally intelligent'.

On finding the shirt Federica places it into her bag and immediately begins to leave the store. As she does, another figure walks onto the screen – or rather in front of her. 'Do you have everything you need today Ms Antonietta? How was the tracksuit you bought in February? We have something similar for winter – would you like me to send it to Alex for you to look at?'

'Please, that would be wonderful,' Federica says. 'I don't want to be late.' She leaves the store, and the RFID tag on the shirt automatically debits her account. In the production, warehousing, distribution and sale of the item, not one human was employed. Indeed, the store she visited could have delivered it by drone to her nephew later that day, but she preferred giving it to him herself – the old-fashioned way. After all, it's a birthday present from his favourite aunt.

Doug

Doug had both known this would happen and prayed that it wouldn't. He just wanted to take his dog for a walk and now it was going to be put down.

'Sir, I'm going to have to take the animal.'

'Why?' asks Doug. 'I have a licence for it – what did I do wrong?'

'It's a counterfeit item, sir. If you do have a licence it will be a forgery – you are either handling illegally edited goods or … you've done this yourself.'

Doug had bought the dog, a Dachshund he'd named Noodle, from a breeder who had a reputation for dealing with upgraded animals. He had taken the risk because he didn't want something that might lose the use of its back legs after a few years – he'd had a pug in the past and as much as he loved it, it could barely breathe at night. If he had to have another animal that screwed up again – his apartment was too small for even a moderately sized dog – he wouldn't have bothered at all. 'Give me a break. These animals have been bred to fuck by us, we made them like this, and now you are saying it's illegal to put that right?'

'So you are aware of the edits, sir?' asks the policeman, putting away his gene tracker and beginning to tap on his tablet.

'No I wasn't, and you won't be able to prove something that hasn't happened … it's just I find all this nonsense of scanning for "Frankenstein" animals and crops and people … it's fucking ridiculous.'

'It's the law, sir. If we didn't have these rules in place, then where would the incentive be for people to create new solutions? People could just do anything they wanted.'

'Or heal anything they wanted,' Doug muttered.

The police officer remained completely indifferent. 'Now sir, may I take your name, address and a shot of your retina … stand still, this won't take a moment.'

All of the accounts above are fiction, and yet they are based in fact – reasonable guesses about our prospective future. In

2015 Barack Obama, then US president, signed the SPACE Act into law. Less than two years later, Kaua'i, the fourth largest of the Hawai'ian Islands, finalised a deal with Solar City allowing the island to meet its entire electricity needs from solar power. Around the same time, technology entrepreneur Mark Cuban declared that the world's first trillionaire would emerge in the space of artificial intelligence.

In Seattle, meanwhile, Amazon trialled its first checkout-free store using 'just walk out technology'. Almost simultaneously, Foxconn's CEO, Terry Gou, announced the construction of a major facility by the company in Wisconsin. Eight hundred miles south in the state of Mississippi, David Ishee, a dog breeder and biohacker, was refused permission by the FDA to edit the genome of dogs he bred in order to eliminate a specific but common condition. His response? That he might do it anyway as an act of civil disobedience. A year after that FDA ruling, in February 2018, SpaceX oversaw the successful launch, re-entry and landing of its Falcon Heavy rocket – the predecessor to the BFR booster the company intends to deploy in its manned missions to Mars in the 2020s.

All of these events share a certain sense of the future. Renewable energy, asteroid mining, rockets which can be used multiple times and even fly to Mars, industry leaders openly discussing the implications of AI, DIY enthusiasts immersing themselves in low-cost genetic engineering. And yet, that future is already here. It turns out it isn't tomorrow's world which is too complex to craft a meaningful politics for, it's today's.

In attempting to create a progressive politics that fits to present realities this poses a problem because, while these events feel like something from science fiction, they can also feel inevitable. In one sense it's like the future is already written, and that for all the talk of an impending technological revolution, such dizzying transformation is attached to a static view of the world where nothing really changes.

But what if everything could change? What if, more than simply meeting the great challenges of our time – from climate change to inequality and ageing – we went far beyond them, putting today's problems behind us like we did before with large predators and, for the most part, illness. What if, rather than having no sense of a different future, we decided history hadn't actually begun?

We have faced changes as momentous as those which now confront us twice before. The first was around twelve thousand years ago as *Homo sapiens*, our ancestors, began to engage in agriculture for the first time. This consisted in the domestication of animals and crops, practically grasping how biological features can be bred both in and out of species. It wasn't long before we had farming, animals performing labour and a relative abundance of food. This in turn created the social surplus necessary for the transition to sedentary society and with it cities, writing and culture. In short, life would never be the same again. This was both the end of something – hundreds of millennia of human 'prehistory' – and the start of something else.

It was the First Disruption.

After that not much would change for thousands of years. Yes, there was progress, as civilisations emerged and empires conquered, but fundamentally, the same sources of light, energy and warmth were available five thousand years ago as five hundred years ago. Life expectancy depended more on geography, social status and war than on technology and, until the last few centuries, most people's 'work' involved subsistence agriculture.

Then, around the middle of the eighteenth century, a new

transformation began. The steam engine – along with coal – became the backbone of the Industrial Revolution and the first machine age. While it had taken all of recorded history for the world's human population to reach 1 billion, it would take little more than a century to double once more. Now, new vistas of abundance opened up, with extended life expectancy, near-universal literacy, and increased production of just about everything. By the middle of the nineteenth century it was once again clear that something so seismic had taken place that, for better or worse, there was no going back.

This was the Second Disruption.

The present conjuncture offers a rupture just as significant as these two earlier moments. As with the Second Disruption it will offer relative liberation from scarcity in vital areas – energy, cognitive labour and information rather than simply the mechanical power of the Industrial Revolution. As with the First it will signal a departure from all history before it, heralding a beginning more than a final destination.

But this Third Disruption – now in its opening decades – is still to be contested, and its consequences remain uncertain. While the forces underpinning it are already present – as will be highlighted over the following chapters – an appropriate politics remains unclear. Importantly, its possibilities are such that they call into question some of the basic assumptions of our social and economic system. Thus, far from being confronted with a choice between change and inertia, a world dramatically different from our own is both inevitable and near at hand. The key question is this one: In whose interests will it be created?

What follows is a summary of the world in which this has begun to unfold, presenting the spectre of crisis – ecological, economic and social – alongside the potential abundance of an emerging alternative. From there it is proposed that a political map can be gleaned from both the challenges we face and the potential tools at our disposal. This map is Fully Automated Luxury Communism.

After the realm of speculation, we draw upon the world as it is, or rather as it is becoming. Here we examine seemingly disparate technologies – in automation, energy, resources, health and food – before concluding that the foundations are cohering for a society beyond both scarcity and work. Nothing is certain about where these technologies will end, nor whose benefit they will serve. What is discernible, however, is that a disposition can be drawn from them – if only they are allied to a political project of collective solidarity and individual happiness.

This is why Fully Automated Luxury Communism (FALC) is a politics rather than some inevitable future. To that end, it requires a strategy for our times while carving new figureheads for utopia, outlining the world as it could be and where to begin.

So let us start at the end – or so we thought – with the strange death of the future.

I.
Chaos under Heaven

1
The Great Disorder

'How did you go bankrupt?' Bill asked.
'Two ways,' Mike said. 'Gradually and then suddenly.'

Ernest Hemingway, *The Sun Also Rises*

In the summer of 1989, as it became clear the United States and its allies had won the Cold War, Francis Fukuyama wrote an essay titled 'The End of History?' for the *National Interest*.

Its core proposition was provocative yet simple, with the little-known academic asserting that the collapse of the Soviet Union was of greater importance than simply marking the end of a military rivalry: 'What we may be witnessing is not just the end of the Cold War, or the passing of a particular period of postwar history, but the end of history as such: that is, the end point of mankind's ideological evolution and the universalization of Western liberal democracy as the final form of human government.'

Fukuyama's contention was that, while clocks would still tick and years continue to roll by, no new ideas would emerge, at least none capable of challenging the status quo. In making this extraordinary claim, he referenced the unlikely authorities of Karl Marx and Georg Wilhelm Friedrich Hegel. In their different ways both had claimed that history had a final destination. Now, with the end of the Cold War, they were proven right – only rather than the Prussian state or the downfall of capitalism, the twilight of ideology was Big Macs and Coca-Cola.

Fukuyama swiftly became an intellectual superstar, turning the essay into his first book *The End of History and the Last Man*, published in 1992. There he offered an extended explanation of his core hypothesis from three years earlier, outlining how history is primarily driven by ideas constantly competing with one another. As a result, by the 1990s liberal democracy, and by extension market capitalism, reigned supreme because no viable alternative remained. While in a sense that was true – the USSR had just disintegrated – it failed to grasp how the gravest challenges are more likely to emerge from internal contradiction or external, unanticipated, shock than an absence of consent.

For Fukuyama the end of history signalled a world defined by economic calculation and 'the endless solving of technical problems, environmental concerns, and the satisfaction of sophisticated consumer demands'. And yet the present moment, defined by challenges such as rising temperatures, technological unemployment, income inequality and societal ageing – to name just a few – poses questions which extend beyond mere technical competence. If Fukuyama's words were naive in 1992, then in the decade that followed the financial crisis of 2008 they became positively ridiculous. Indeed, he admitted as much in a book he published on identity in 2018.

But the stakes are greater than simply being right or wrong on an issue of academic detail. Because worse than naive credulity or mistaking a brief moment for historic permanence, many in power still view Fukuyama's hypothesis as sacrosanct. Three decades after the end of the Cold War the legacy of his work is a political 'common sense' that actively obstructs us from addressing the great challenges we face. After all, why would decisive action – particularly if it undermined the interests of business and profit – be necessary if nothing really changes?

Fukuyama's triumphalist thinking a generation ago, even if he himself has now renounced it somewhat, still matters. That is because it has since gone on to infuse a broader folk politics that understood the end of the Cold War to not only signify the supremacy of market capitalism, but also the inevitable demise of self-governing nation-states.

In this flat, crowded and connected world everything would be subject to ever-accelerating change. Everything, that is, except the rules of the game. Indeed, many no longer even considered them to be rules but rather reality itself, with alternative political systems viewed as either futile or incomprehensible. Here, liberal capitalism went from a contingent project to a reality principle. Welcome to the world of capitalist realism – where the map is the territory and nothing really matters.

Capitalist Realism

Capitalist realism is best summed up with a single sentence: 'It is easier to imagine the end of the world than the end of capitalism.'*

For Mark Fisher – the British theorist who coined the term – that catchphrase captures the very essence of our era, with

---

* This phrase is attributed to both Fredric Jameson and Slavoj Žižek, although Jameson himself is unclear as to its original source.

capitalism not only viewed as the exclusively 'viable political and economic system' but also one where it is 'impossible even to imagine a coherent alternative'. After all, how can you contrive an alternative to reality itself?

Turning to the 2006 film *Children of Men*, Fisher investigates its surreal normality as a dystopia fit for our age with the world it projects 'more like an extrapolation or exacerbation of ours (rather) than an alternative to it. In its world, as in ours, ultra-authoritarianism and Capital are by no means incompatible: internment camps and franchise coffee bars co-exist.'

This tallies with the thinking of Alain Badiou, who writes,

> We live in a contradiction … where all existence … is presented to us as ideal. To justify their conservatism, the partisans of the established order cannot really call it ideal or wonderful. So instead, they have decided to say that all the rest is horrible … our democracy is not perfect. But it's better than the bloody dictatorships. Capitalism is unjust. But it's not criminal like Stalinism. We let millions of Africans die of AIDS, but we don't make racist nationalist declarations like Milosevic.

Because capitalist realism has no offer of a better future – especially so over the course of the last decade – its default logic is one of anti-utopianism. Flat wages, falling home ownership and a warming planet might be bad, granted, but at least we have iPhones. And, yes, you may not be able to access the things your parents took for granted, like affordable homes or free higher education, but you should still be grateful – at least it's not the sixteenth century.

Over time this argument, seductive for the opening years of the twenty-first century, is being revealed as patently absurd. Capitalist realism, a world where nothing really changes, is giving way to a historic moment defined by crisis. One where, unless we transform our understanding of the future once more, the very worst demons of centuries past will prevail.

Crisis Unleashed

To say the present era is one of crisis borders on cliché. Habitual and familiar, this crisis differs from the dystopias of George Orwell or Aldous Huxley, or hell in the paintings of Bosch or the last days of Earth as told in the Book of Revelations. It is unlike Europe during the Black Death or Central Asia as it faced the galloping Golden Horde. Here, instead, we inhabit a world in free-fall and yet we are all along for the ride.

Some aspects of this, like the European migration crisis, are highly mediatised and public. Here, people displaced by war and social breakdown migrate, often meeting with hostility in response. While for previous generations the Berlin Wall was totemic of division, only 235 people died trying to cross it. Compare that to the 3,770 souls who died or went missing in the Mediterranean trying to reach the shores of Europe just in 2015. And if, as an undocumented migrant, you are fortunate enough to safely cross the Mediterranean, or the US–Mexico border, or the fences and forests between Hungary and Bulgaria, your problems are only just beginning.

There are of course other expressions of our broken world that are equally profound, if less immediately obvious. One is a crisis of mental health, with suicide the leading killer of British men under the age of fifty and depression expected to be the leading cause of the global burden of disease by 2030.

Others still are less easy to personalise, remaining incomprehensible on a human scale. One is a crisis of the state, as agency ebbs to the market and an increasingly globalised economy undermines the ability of nations to act decisively. This process of market and capital integration – where commodities move more seamlessly than ever – is entirely at odds with the experience of displaced peoples and undocumented migrants as they face walls, surveillance and ever more securitised borders.

As the state gives way to the market this is accompanied by a nebulous sense of loss, as a crisis of representation empties democratic institutions of authority and citizens come to view them as little more than conduits for the interests of corrupt elites. This entrenches the tendencies of globalisation as previous, if imperfect, repositories of accountability – national governments – lose the consent of those they represent. In the supposedly good times something had gone badly wrong – but it remained an undercurrent.

2008: Return of History

Almost two decades after Fukuyama's false prophecy, that decisively changed: a banking crisis, a debt crisis, a deficit crisis – all culminating in the imposition of austerity, from Greece to California. Alongside that was war in Georgia, the flowering of the Arab Spring, uprising in the Ukraine, insurrection – and then the most bloody of civil wars – in Syria. Elsewhere previously low-intensity conflict in Iraq and Afghanistan deteriorated further, soon joined by similarly hazy struggles in Libya and Yemen. In early 2014 the Russian Federation added new territory for the first time as it annexed Crimea following a local referendum. A few months later, straddling Syria and Iraq in an area the size of the United Kingdom, insurgents declared a caliphate, the Islamic State.

But even amid all this it was events in Western Europe, a heartland of capitalist realism, which proved most surprising:

a heightened cycle of protest and riot in England after 2010 was followed by a failed but surprisingly close referendum on Scottish independence four years later. Even that paled into insignificance, however, when in 2016 Britain voted to leave the European Union, becoming the first member-state in its history to do so.

While 'Brexit' was the most important political moment in Europe for a generation, it was soon outdone by events across the Atlantic when, just a few months later, Donald Trump was elected the forty-fifth president of the United States. Less than a decade after the collapse of Lehman Brothers in 2008, it was now undeniable. An expansionist Russia, isolationist Britain and broken economic model had all been outdone by a reality TV star becoming the most powerful person on Earth. History was back.

Trump's inauguration speech the following February stood in defiant contrast to the heady rhetoric of his predecessor, Barack Obama, when he assumed office eight years earlier. Claiming that the system was failing ordinary Americans, Trump's explicit message of social decay and aggrieved nationalism became his immediate signature in office.

And yet in a strange way, despite their markedly different forms of presentation, Obama and Trump shared a similar faith in the unique ability of markets to find solutions. After all, anything else is tantamount to heresy in a world of capitalist realism – where the end of the world is more plausible than the end of capitalism.

This condition presents arguably the most pressing crisis of all: an absence of collective imagination. It is as if all humanity has been afflicted by a psychological complex, capitalist realism making us believe the present world is stronger than our capacity to remake it – as if it were not our ancestors who created what stands before us now. As if the very essence of humanity, if there is such a thing, is not to constantly build new worlds.

In its defence, capitalism can point to an impressive record, at least so far. Having faced crises almost every decade for two centuries, amid the ferocious pace of constantly accelerating change, it has always found ways of extracting profit and, eventually, improving living standards. Capitalism has survived, evolved and prospered through the Industrial Revolution, the Great Depression, protectionism, two World Wars, the end of the gold standard and the demise of the Bretton Woods Agreement. Little more than a generation ago, much of the world was under the political influence of the former Soviet Union, with it and the United States seemingly destined to face off in nuclear confrontation. And yet that never came to pass and, as Fukuyama would later write, a divided world was replaced by one where markets prevailed and liberal democracy would reign supreme.

This explains why, in spite of manifest crises, those who champion the status quo are as confident as they are. Ours may well be a world of low growth, declining living standards and rising geopolitical tensions, but capitalism's staunchest advocates draw strength from knowing similar problems have been dealt with before.

But besides those issues are challenges seemingly harder to overcome. In isolation each is historically significant, yet taken together they can be viewed as threats whose scale is civilisational, holding the potential to undermine the ability of capitalism to reproduce itself as a system based on infinite growth, production for profit and wage-labour.

There are five such crises, which at times overlap. They are climate change and the consequences of global warming; resource scarcity – particularly for energy, minerals and fresh water; societal ageing, as life expectancy increases and birth rates concurrently fall; a growing surplus of global poor who form an ever-larger 'unnecessariat'; and, perhaps most critically, a new machine age which will herald ever-greater technological unemployment as progressively more physical and cognitive labour is performed by machines, rather than humans.

Confronting such crises is the basis of FALC. Capitalism, at least as we know it, is about to end. What matters is what comes next.

The claim that *capitalism will end*, is, for capitalist realism, like saying a triangle doesn't have three sides or that the law of gravity no longer applies while an apple falls from a tree. Rather than understanding the present as one historical period among many, like Victorian England or the Roman Republic, to be alive at the end of history means presuming our social systems to be as unchanging as the physical laws that govern the universe.

And yet the truth is capitalist realism is already coming apart. The fact you are reading these words at all is proof.

Despite the observations of Francis Fukuyama and his disciples, history returned on 15 September 2008 when the global financial system crashed. Within weeks the world's leading economic powers, previous zealots for minimal state interference, were left with no alternative but to bail out their domestic banks, with some even being nationalised. That exposed their previous free market fervour for the lie it was: this was socialism for the rich and market capitalism for the rest. The critics had always said as much, now nobody could deny it.

But as well as revealing what had passed as common sense for the political project it was, that moment also ended a phase of global expansion that had powered financial services and real estate – most notably in Britain and the United States – to the forefront of economic life. Over the preceding two decades it was these areas which had underpinned growth, tax receipts and forms of asset ownership which were at least moderately distributed. After 2008 that decisively changed, meaning that in many countries poverty has increased, wages have stagnated and growth – in any significant sense – has vanished.

In the US the Supplemental Nutrition Assistance Program, popularly known as 'food stamps', is a federal initiative that helps low-income Americans buy food. By virtue of its objective it is one of the most accurate indicators of poverty in the country. While in 2007, immediately before the crisis, 26 million Americans were in receipt of food stamps, by 2012 – at the tail end of what some now call 'the Great Recession' – that figure had almost doubled to 46 million. Over subsequent years, despite an alleged upturn in the country's economic fortunes, that number barely moved, with Donald Trump frequently highlighting how 43 million Americans used food stamps while on the campaign trail in 2016. For all the talk of his victory being powered by 'fake news', that number was entirely accurate.

Analogous to food stamp use in the US is the meteoric rise in the number of people using food banks in Britain. The Trussell Trust, which operates the largest food bank network in the country, claims to have delivered around 41,000 food packs in 2010. By 2017 that had risen to 1.2 million after nine consecutive years of rising demand for their services. While the increased use of food banks in the UK is partially the result of disastrous welfare reforms, it also reflects something observable on both sides of the Atlantic: being in work no longer guarantees escaping poverty – quite the opposite.

The most detailed data available in the UK only serves to

confirm a historic shift has taken place over the last decade, with those in relative poverty more likely to be in a working household than not. Most troubling of all is that this is accelerating: by the end of 2016, 55 per cent of people in poverty were in a household where someone was employed – an astonishing 7.4 million people. Just six months later that figure had risen to 60 per cent.

Powering this downward spiral is falling wages: since 2008, real pay in Britain, which takes inflation into account, has dropped by more than 10 per cent. It should come as little surprise, then, that nearly 17 million Brits of working age have less than £100 in personal savings. In the United States it's a similar story, with 63 per cent of Americans saying they have $500 or less put aside.

The other pillar of consent for twentieth-century capitalism, of property-ownership as the complement to democracy, is in similar retreat. In Britain, where the Conservative Noel Skelton coined the term 'property-owning democracy' in 1923, home-ownership is at its lowest level since 1985 and continues to fall. It's even worse in the US, though, where a combination of high prices, low wages and little credit means the average American is less likely to own their own home than at any time since 1965 – four years before the Moon landing.

Measuring Inertia

While ordinary people are struggling, measured through use of food banks and food stamps, wages which buy less or unmet expectations regarding home ownership, the abstract vision of the economy pedalled by elites, defined by growth and productivity, is in similar disarray. After all, on output per hour worked, perhaps the most useful measure of economic progress, Britain produced less in 2017 than it did a decade earlier. Such a development is without precedent in modern history.

Similar issues are in evidence elsewhere around the world. 'Lost decade', previously used to describe anomalous economic conditions in countries like Italy and Japan, is increasingly applied to an ever-growing cluster of nations. Since the crisis of 2008, Greece and Spain have seen unemployment go beyond 25 per cent, with youth unemployment touching double that. Elsewhere, economies such as Hungary, Austria, Portugal and Latvia's are no bigger now than they were in 2008 when measured on an output-per-person basis.

Even in the rising nations of the Global South, the trend is clear. The 10 per cent growth which characterised the Chinese and Indian economies during the early years of the twenty-first century are now a thing of the past. Elsewhere the likes of Brazil and Russia have been mired in recession almost as severe as parts of Europe, the only difference being their economic malaise has kicked in at far lower levels of relative development. Such a shift has only served to strengthen the forces of autocracy.

So our world is one increasingly defined by low growth, low productivity and low wages. Before the crisis, most policy-makers would have thought such events impossible, let alone speculated about an appropriate response. Alan Greenspan's 2008 remarks to the US House of Representatives are illustrative: the banking crisis having left this former chairman of the Federal Reserve in a state of 'shocked disbelief' and 'distressed' by events he previously viewed as impossible.

While neoliberalism, which emerged with the Thatcher and Reagan governments, led to higher unemployment and lower wage growth, for more than a generation this was mitigated by access to cheaper goods and services – by relocating production to countries with lower wages – as well as inflated asset prices, particularly housing, and access to cheap mortgage and consumer debt. As well as forming the foundation for a widely felt material improvement in living standards, this was the economic base for a world where there was no alternative. How could you *really* be angry at anything with your credit cards and ever-cheaper consumer gadgets? And even if you were, what choice did you have once you'd earned your stake in the system with a home of your own? Now, with these previous fixtures in retreat, elites have yet to make a positive offer about what comes next. What we know for certain is that the status quo can't hold. There is no consent for a system which, on nearly every measure, is going backwards.

This all explains the revival of radical politics, on both the left and right, in recent years. Because the events of 2008 came as such a shock – even for the system's outsiders – nobody proved immediately able to take advantage of such a historic opportunity. Gradually that would change, however, with the previously unthinkable becoming increasingly commonplace. In the 2009 European Parliamentary elections, the far right made impressive gains across the continent with the likes of UKIP, France's Front National and even the British National Party attracting widespread support. The BNP's results in particular came as a shock, with a party historically connected to the country's neo-Nazi movement gaining almost 1 million votes and two MEPs. For a few years similar energies on the left were limited to the streets – such as the 2010 British student movement and the Spanish Indignados – but eventually these too translated to success at the ballot box. Spain offered the most obvious initial expression of that with the emergence of a new party, Podemos, which gained five MEPs in 2014 just a few months after it had been formed, before finishing third in the following year's Spanish general election.

But before then, in January 2015, Greece's Syriza, a coalition of previously insignificant left-wing groups, would win the most seats in that country's general election. After agreeing to be the senior partner in a wider coalition they formed a government, becoming the first party of the radical left to do so in a Western democracy since the Second World War. This fed hopes of a deal between Greece and the 'Troika' of the European Commission, European Central Bank and the International Monetary Fund on the terms of their coming bailout deal that summer. In due course Syriza campaigned for an 'Oxi' vote, defying the conditions proposed by the Troika. To widespread amazement, oxi – no in Greek – won by a landslide. While the Troika would refuse to change their stance in the negotiations that followed, and the Greek government capitulated to their terms, a new reality had emerged: the corridors of power were no longer insulated from mass protest in the streets.

In Britain, meanwhile, the Conservative Party won its first majority since 1992 as the right-wing UKIP attracted almost 4 million votes and the Scottish National Party took an astonishing forty seats from Labour in Scotland. A few months later, Jeremy Corbyn, who began his outsider bid at odds of 200–1, became Leader of the Labour Party – his supporters certain he could be powered by the same wave that had taken the likes of Syriza and Podemos so far in such a short space of time.

It was 2016 which proved to be the decisive year, however, as a crisis that started eight years earlier found its most potent political expressions. In June, Britain voted to leave the European Union with more people voting in the 'Brexit' referendum than any previous vote held in the country. That appeared to be a pivotal moment, with right-wing populism seeming to capture an increasingly clear hostility to governing elites. As Nigel Farage, a figurehead for the Brexit movement, triumphantly declared on the night, 'This is a victory for ordinary people, for good people, for decent people ... the people who've had enough of the merchant bankers.'

Yet even the shock of Brexit paled in comparison to events just a few months later when Donald Trump, a well-known businessman and reality TV star, was elected president of the United States. Winning the Republican primary earlier that year had already caused a shock – and with Bernie Sanders pushing Hillary Clinton close for the Democratic nomination, the signs were there for an upset. Which was precisely what ensued as Trump took previously democrat-held 'Rust Belt' states on his way to the White House. The President-elect's victory speech was reminiscent of Farage's, as he told 'the forgotten men and women of our country' that they would be 'forgotten no longer'.

The following April, buoyed by the perception of a zeitgeist seemingly to her advantage, Britain's new Prime Minister Theresa May called a general election to cement her party's grip on power. An enhanced majority was widely viewed as inevitable, the question being how big a landslide the Conservatives could achieve. And yet, in a manner analogous to both Trump and Brexit, Labour defied the odds with a clear message of a break with the status quo. While they didn't form a government, they did deprive the Tories of a majority, winning an additional 3.5 million votes in the process and enjoying the biggest increase in vote share – for any party – since 1945. The Tories, significantly to the right of their campaigns in recent years also did well, winning their highest share of the vote since 1987. Britain now displayed both key features of the new political landscape: massively increased polarisation, and uncertainty as to whether the politics of the left or right would ultimately prevail.

While they might not share much politically, Trump and Corbyn, along with Brexit and the emergence of Podemos, Bernie Sanders and Syriza, indicate the era of capitalist realism is over.

And yet there is also a deeper story at play, one which remains largely unremarked upon. While the events of the last several years are both historic and unexpected, they are a response to an economic crisis, beginning in 2008, which itself only represents the first stage of a prolonged period of global disorder. Over coming decades we will not only endure the aftershocks of the failure of this economic model to deliver rising living standards, but also the era-defining effects of the aforementioned five crises. Individually, each poses an existential threat to our way of life. Together they could blow away the social and economic certainties of the last two and a half centuries.

But there is a deeper layer still, because we are at a crossroads as much as a cliff edge. Alongside these challenges we also see the contours of something new, a society as distinct from our own as that of the twentieth century to feudalism, or urban civilisation from the life of the hunter-gatherer. It builds on technologies whose development has been accelerating for decades which, only now, are set to undermine the key features of everything we had previously presumed to be as unchanging as scarcity itself.

Its name? Fully automated luxury communism.

2

The Three Disruptions

Technology is a gift of God. After the gift of life it is perhaps the greatest of God's gifts.

Freeman Dyson

Agriculture: The First Disruption

While change is history's only constant, some changes matter more than others. Indeed some are so powerful that they alter the very meaning of what it is to be human – making an imprint so profound we can never return to the way things were before.

In this respect, two changes – what shall be called disruptions – stand out in particular.

The first disruption took place around twelve thousand years ago as our ancestors transitioned from nomadic hunting and gathering to a life of settled agriculture. Referred to as the Neolithic revolution, this shift, powered by the innovation of domesticating animals and plants, generated something never known before: a sizeable surplus of food and energy. For the first time in their existence, humans could begin to think about the future and make plans for a world that would be different to the one around them. The realms of abstract thought and practical action increasingly overlapped.

Over subsequent generations, and through constant modification of the natural environment, these settlements became ever more populated – capable of sustaining higher densities of people. Slowly, a world recognisable to us emerged: labour began to specialise, bringing along with it trade, the development of arts, centralised administration, codified systems of knowledge such as writing and mathematics, and various forms of property. It was during this period that the human animal asserted its mastery above all others, its existence increasingly defined by an ability to deploy complex technologies alongside sophisticated social institutions. All of this was built upon the shift to agriculture – the foundation of the First Disruption.

Industry: The Second Disruption

The second change was more recent, and certainly easier to locate. Beginning around 250 years ago, what has been termed the 'First Machine Age' gave the world the Industrial Revolution. Just as the earlier development of agriculture transformed human society, industry allowed previously unimaginable feats of both creation and destruction.

This Second Disruption was powered as much by a transformation in energy as it was in production. Even as late as the 1600s – the century of Isaac Newton and Galileo – the primary sources of power remained much the same as in antiquity: water, wind, animals and humans. While there had been an energy revolution in medieval Europe, centred around the vertical windmill, this was unevenly distributed and far from exercising a regional, let alone global, impact.

Yet all of that changed over the next 150 years. Increasingly efficient engines powered by fossil fuels untied economic production from organic labour and unreliable forms of renewable energy. The general-purpose technology on which this was based was steam power, the first commercial application of which was Thomas Newcomen's 1712 atmospheric engine. And yet it wasn't until the closing decades of the century that capturing the power of steam proved transformational. While the steam engine was not a new creation, an improved version designed by James Watt turned it from a tool of marginal use to the focal point of what became the Industrial Revolution. Just as with agriculture twelve thousand years earlier, this was a shift so big that there was no reverse gear.

The consequences of all of this were extraordinary. The combination of steam power and fossil fuels re-oriented production around the factory system, and allowed the creation of national and global infrastructures through railway networks and ocean-going steamships. In 1830, less than two decades after the railway locomotive had been designed, the world's first intercity route opened between Liverpool and Manchester. Another twenty years after that, Great Britain was home to over 7,000 miles of railway lines used by more than 48 million people annually.

Although Britain was at the forefront of such change, such trends rapidly went global. Thus while it was conceivable in 1873 that Phileas Fogg, the protagonist of Jules Verne's *Around the World in Eighty Days*, could circumnavigate the world in under three months, the same journey took more than a year only a generation earlier. This unprecedented contraction of space and time would have particularly profound implications for the world's rising economic superpower, the United States. In 1847, the journey from New York to Chicago took at least three weeks by stagecoach. A decade later, the same trip by rail took three days.

With the rise of global transportation networks came international, real-time forms of communication. In 1865 the first transatlantic telegraph cable was laid between Britain and the United States. By the early 1870s the same technology connected London and Adelaide on opposite sides of the world. In 1871 the results of the Derby, the prestigious horse race, were flashed from London to Calcutta in five minutes, putting to shame the eighty days of Verne's travelling adventurer. All of this – global transport, electricity, rapid communication – would have been impossible to predict when Watt patented his first engine with Matthew Boulton a century earlier.

Capitalism's Critics

Alongside the emergence of a global economy with new forms of transit and communication, the technologies of the Second Disruption significantly entrenched the division of labour, making new kinds of abundance possible. The incremental substitution of natural by mechanical power, combined with open markets and global competition, significantly reduced the numbers of those engaged in artisanal work, displacing craft from the centre of the human experience to its margins. Perhaps paradoxically this made previously unthinkable feats of ingenuity an almost mundane feature of life. Even Marx, a profound critic of the new system, was in awe when he wrote in 1848:

> The bourgeoisie ... has been the first to show what man's activity can bring about. It has accomplished wonders far surpassing Egyptian pyramids, Roman aqueducts, and Gothic cathedrals; it has conducted expeditions that put in the shade all former Exoduses of nations and crusades.

For Marx, however, these new industrial feats were just the tip of the iceberg. He believed that such changes in technology, production and social life, would come to form the basis of an entirely new society. This reflected his view of history as unfolding through an ensemble of fields encompassing not only technology, but also politics and our ideas and assumptions about both the world and each other. Technology – just as it had done twelve thousand years earlier with the First Disruption – had ushered humanity into a new paradigm, yet we remained unable to create the institutions and ideas appropriate for this new age. Achieving that was the project to which Marx would commit his life.

In contrast to his portrayal by critics, Marx was often lyrical about capitalism. His belief was that despite its capacity for exploitation, its compulsion to innovate – along with the creation of a world market – forged the conditions for social transformation:

> The bourgeoisie cannot exist without constantly revolutionising the instruments of production, and thereby the relations of production, and with them the whole relations of society ... constant revolutionising of production, uninterrupted disturbance of all social conditions, everlasting uncertainty and agitation distinguish the bourgeois epoch from all earlier ones.

As a result, his conclusion was that capitalism inevitably 'created its own gravediggers':

> The condition for capital is wage-labour. Wage-labour rests exclusively on competition between the labourers. The advance of industry, whose involuntary promoter is the bourgeoisie, replaces the isolation of the labourers, due to competition, by the revolutionary combination, due to association.

And yet this never came to pass. There was never a workers' revolution that overthrew the system – at least not on a global scale. The reason why was that contrary to Marx's predictions capitalism could 'fix' – both spatially and technologically – the very problems it generated. The 'spatial fix' is what underpins contemporary globalisation, characterised by the global distribution and relocation of production. This was one of the solutions the bourgeoisie adopted to counter rising worker militancy in Europe and North America after the late 1960s, and is the background for contemporary discourses of 'competitive' labour markets in a world 'racing to the bottom'. It is also why more cars are produced in Mexico, Thailand and Brazil than nations which previously dominated the industry such as France, Italy and the United Kingdom. The spatial fix is always only temporary, of course, and has recently re-emerged in the context of rising wages in China. Once more we see production relocating to wherever labour is cheap and profits easier to realise.

The 'technological fix' is different, with Marx consistently clear that technological innovation is an inherent feature of capitalism. His explanation, just as it would be for later voices such as Milton Friedman and Joseph Schumpeter, was that it was propelled by competition between capitalists. The imperative to compete means capitalists must always find cheaper, more efficient ways of producing commodities – often substituting machines for human labour – while also offering improvements on goods and services available to consumers. It was this imperative which governed the immense expansion of railways, the emergence of the factory system and guided constant innovation until the present day. It would become the iron law of the prevailing economic model within the Second Disruption – market capitalism.

Information Unbound: The Third Disruption

This tendency to perpetually innovate as a result of competition, to constantly supplant work performed by humans and maximise productivity, would ultimately lead to a Third Disruption, one whose fullest conclusions are no less dizzying than the two which preceded it.

This Third Disruption has already started, with evidence of its arrival all around us. As with the Second Disruption its basis is a general-purpose technology: the modern transistor and integrated circuit, contemporary analogues to Watt's steam engine over two centuries ago.

While the Second Disruption was marked by a relative freedom from scarcity in motive power – coal and oil rather than muscle and wind moving wheels, pulleys, ships, people and goods – the defining feature of the Third Disruption is ever-greater abundance in information. For some this signals the completion of the Industrial Revolution, marking an era in which machines are increasingly able to perform cognitive as well as physical tasks.

This new situation of post-scarcity underpins what will be referred to as 'extreme supply', something not only limited to information, but – as a consequence of digitisation – labour too. Here, continuous improvements in processor power, in combination with a range of other technologies, means machines will be capable of replicating ever more of what was, until now, uniquely human work.

As with preceding disruptions, this shift represents a transformation in energy as much as work. Just as the First Disruption depended on the energy of domesticated animals, humans and the elements, and the Second was powered by the condensed solar energy of fossil fuels, the Third Disruption sees a move away from hydrocarbons and back to renewable energy – particularly solar. This will partially be a response to the perils of climate change, but as with other features of the Third Disruption its tendency to extreme supply is more profound than the simple pursuit of sustainability. It will spell an end to energy scarcity altogether, as a new technology-energy matrix of ever-smarter machines combined with ever-cheaper and cleaner energy will make resource extraction beyond our world possible, yielding extreme supply in raw materials. This completes a chain that permits humanity to entirely exceed our present limits.

In a sense this abundance is befitting of nature and our solar system. While we are accustomed to thinking of work as necessary and energy as a scarce resource, there is literally nothing on our planet so plentiful as the power of our sun. In the span of just ninety minutes enough potential solar energy hits the Earth's surface to meet present demand for an entire year. Every twelve months we receive twice as much energy from the sun as will ever be obtained from the entirety of Earth's non-renewable sources – coal, oil, natural gas and mined uranium – combined. While rising global demand for energy might seem daunting, it is nothing compared to what the giant nuclear reactor approximately 149 million kilometres away can provide.

Such unearthly wealth is only matched by the mineral resources beyond our planet, particularly among near Earth asteroids (NEA). Take the asteroid 16 Psyche, located in the belt between Mars and Jupiter. Measuring over 200 kilometres in diameter, it is one of the largest asteroids in our solar system. Composed of iron, nickel and rarer metals such as copper, gold and platinum, its iron content alone could be worth $10,000 quadrillion – not bad when you consider the annual GDP of the Earth economy stands at around $80 trillion. Psyche is unique, but it demonstrates a crucial point: the opportunities of off-world mining – once the technical barriers are surmounted – are as breathtaking as machines that can perform any task, or the sun sustaining our cities as it presently does our forests and fields.

Biology as Information

The implications of extreme supply in information extend beyond automation. Ultimately, we will encounter new possibilities in maintaining the biological systems of our planet, as well as feeding and healing our own bodies. And why not? After all, organic life is itself nothing more than encoded information, if a little more complex: there are four nucleobases in double-stranded DNA – C, G, A and T – rather than the binary code of 0s and 1s as with digital information.

So while biological systems are much more complex than any digital equivalent, exponential trends in the latter will enhance our mastery over the former – something which will increasingly resemble an information good. This will transform our relationships to health and lifespan, not to mention food, nature and how we treat our fellow creatures. That doesn't mean we will come to consider any of these to be 'dematerialised'; rather, we will finally grasp the underlying informational rhythms to overcome nearly all forms of disease and feed a world of 10 billion people while using less, rather than more, of our planet's bio-capacity.

Exponential Travel: Understanding the Third Disruption

Given the period between the First and Second Disruptions was some twelve thousand years, it might seem remarkable that the Third comes so soon after Watt's steam engine and the emergence of market capitalism. The explanation why is simple: the rate of historical change is accelerating. The primary driver of that acceleration in recent decades is a number of exponential, as opposed to linear, trends in areas such as the cost of collecting, processing, storing and distributing digital information. It is these exponential trends which underpin extreme supply in information and digitisation, making possible the Third Disruption.

Digitisation is more than simply a process that applies to things like words, pictures, film and music – that these are now digital objects rather than physical ones is important, but not to be overstated. More vital is how digitisation has allowed progressively greater amounts of cognition and memory to be performed in 0s and 1s, with the price–performance ratio of anything that does so falling every year for decades. It is this which allows contemporary camera technology to land rockets and, increasingly, drive autonomous vehicles; it is what will provide robots with fine motor coordination and dexterity equivalent to that found in humans; it will permit the built environment to know more about us, in certain respects, than we know about ourselves. It will even allow us to edit DNA – the building blocks of life – to remove hereditary disease and sequence genomes at such low cost, and with such regularity, that we will cure ourselves of cancer before it reaches Stage 1.

Going Exponential: Ibn Khallikan to Kodak

To better understand how digitisation will shape our future, the story of how photography came to be about 0s and 1s, rather than plastic film, is a good place to start.

While photography went mainstream with the arrival of the first mass-produced camera, Kodak's 1900 'Brownie', the world would have to wait almost a century before the same company released a digital successor. Released in 1991, the DCS 100 enjoyed a maximum resolution of 1.3 megapixels and originally cost $13,000 (around $23,000 today). Despite the stellar price tag restricting its availability to elite institutions and wealthy individuals, the shift to digital was decisive. With photography now an information good, it would exhibit trends analogous to the falling costs and improved price performance described by Moore's Law in computing. As a result, pixels per dollar on commercial digital cameras doubled every year. Just as with computing, the exponential tendencies with digital imaging compounded significantly over time, meaning that the camera on the third generation iPad had a superior resolution by a factor of seven compared to its predecessor, the iPad 2. The significance of this extends beyond the convenience of having affordable consumer cameras. Cheap, ubiquitous cameras are a cornerstone technology in any move towards a society built on automation and data.

The concept of exponential growth, given its rarity in nature, is difficult to immediately grasp. It is most clearly explained in the 'wheat and chessboard problem', first outlined by Ibn Khallikan in the thirteenth century. Some claim this 'problem' was in fact a historical event involving the Emperor of the Gupta Empire and an encounter with the inventor of the game of chess, or a similar precursor.

Supposedly, the Emperor, impressed by the demanding nature of the game he had been shown, told its creator to name their reward. The response he received was as simple as the game was complex: 'place one single grain of rice on the first square of the board, two on the second, four on the third and so on'. With each successive square the number of rice grains was to double – 1, 2, 4, 8, 16, 32 – until the final square of the board was reached. The Emperor, surprised at such a humble request, happily agreed.

It quickly became clear, however, that such a prize was far greater than he had anticipated. After thirty-two squares, only halfway up the board, the game's architect had earned 4 billion grains of rice. While a large number, that was still only equivalent to the amount produced by a large field, and this only served to place the inventor in even higher esteem – after all, a field or two of rice was a perfectly satisfactory reward for such a captivating game. That was to change, though, when by the final square the tally was 18 quintillion grains of rice, a pile larger than Mount Everest and more rice than had been produced in history. The Emperor, enraged by the temerity of a subject who had asked for more wealth than even he could ever offer, ordered the inventor to be executed.

This allegory captures the swift, and often unexpected, dividends of exponential growth, especially compared to linear forms of progress which the human mind is far more inclined to expect. So what happens when such prodigious growth occurs in human affairs? The answer can be found in the history of computing over the last half a century.

In 1965 Gordon Moore, who would later co-found Intel, wrote an article for *Electronics Magazine* detailing recent improvements in the performance of computer chips. At that time the most complex circuit still only had around thirty components, but progress appeared to be accelerating. In fact, Moore observed that the recent rate of development had been so rapid that the number of transistors that could fit on a circuit had doubled every year since 1959. That discovery got him thinking. What would happen if that same trend, of annual doubling, prevailed for another decade?

After some quick calculations, Moore was shocked by the

answer. His forecasts showed that by the end of 1975 the average circuit would have gone from having thirty transistors to 65,000. Moore speculated about the kinds of technology such mesmerising advance could make possible, contemplating a world with 'portable communications equipment', 'home computing' and perhaps even 'automatic controls for automobiles'. Unfortunately for Moore, his prediction proved wildly inaccurate. The trend he outlined didn't persist for another ten years – it's been going for a half century and counting.

When Moore wrote his seminal article, a single transistor spanned the width of a fibre of cotton and cost eight dollars in today's prices. Now, by contrast, billions of transistors can be squeezed onto a chip the size of a fingernail, with a single human hair 10,000 times thicker than Intel's next generation of products. And the cost per unit? That's plummeted too, falling to a tiny fraction of a cent. So while you'll often hear clichés of how modern smartphones are more powerful than the computers used for NASA's Apollo missions, even that fails to convey how dramatically transistors have transformed over the last few decades.

A more useful comparison can be found between the supercomputer ASCI Red and the PlayStation family of games consoles. The former, built by the US government in 1996, was the first machine able to process a teraflop – a trillion floating-point calculations per second. Costing $55 million and measuring the size of a tennis court, its purpose was to predict and model nuclear explosions, something it did with ease as it remained the world's fastest computer until the turn of the millennium – staying in use until as recently as 2005. And yet just one year later, the same processing power was available to consumers in a PlayStation 3, a games console available for as little as $600. The PlayStation 4, released in 2013, was almost twice as powerful as both its predecessor and ASCI Red. Coming in at $400 it cost 1/100,000th of the world's leading supercomputer only two decades earlier.

Such a rapid rate of development is only possible because improvements in processing speed have experienced exponential rather than linear gains over the last sixty years. It is this quality, first observed in computing by Moore, that is powering the Third Disruption far more quickly than many thought possible. Its consequences reach far beyond video games.

While progress over the last half century has been dizzying, the parable of rice grains on the chessboard remains instructive. If such trends persist for another six decades, the results – like the pile of rice bigger than Everest – are almost beyond comprehension. If that single field of rice halfway up the board represents global real-time communication and millions of industrial robots, then what is the mountain?

Can Moore's Law Endure?

The transformative power of Moore's Law, should it persist, is inarguable. The key question, then, is how much longer it can endure. In 2015 researchers at Intel foresaw it prevailing for at least another ten years, although by the standards of a trajectory more than five decades old, that hardly counts as optimistic. A year later William Holt, the company's CEO, was less confident, claiming it might only carry on for another five years and, at best, would significantly slow down thereafter (although he believed progress elsewhere, in areas such as energy efficiency, were likely). That would seem a formidable challenge to more optimistic projections, and if Holt is right our present field of rice will only grow to five or six by the middle of this century. An immense improvement, but certainly not exponential.

Yet there have been Cassandras predicting the demise of Moore's Law for decades. So far they have been proven consistently wrong, with new avenues for improvement opening up just when it seemed any hope for further advance was blocked. Until 2004, increases in the clock speed of chips significantly contributed to enhanced performance, the downside being that overheating placed a limit on how far that innovation could persist. In response, manufacturers incorporated more processor 'cores' as the primary means for accelerating power, with processors now working on different operations in parallel with one another.

It will take similar kinds of innovation to maintain Moore's Law, even if it continues to slow down slightly – something which, in his defence, Holt conceded. While within a decade it may become impossible to miniaturise individual transistors any further, simply because of physical limits, adaptations such as 3-D circuitry and quantum computing – both proven concepts – could mean exponential growth continues. Perhaps even beyond the last square of that chessboard.

More than Processing

Because digitisation is a general-purpose phenomenon, it is not just computer chips that have been subject to its incredible powers of transformation. A similar trend is in evidence with internet bandwidth, where user capacity has grown by between 25 and 50 per cent every year since 1983. The same holds true with data storage, which has likewise enjoyed an exponential function in space-to-cost ratio, with a gigabyte of storage falling from around $200,000 in 1980 to just $0.03 in 2014.

More than anywhere else, however, it is in storage that progress has visibly started to slow down. Even if Toshiba's

3-D Magnetic Recording technology – where a magnetic head writes and reads data on stacked layers using microwaves – is commercially scalable, that would still mean maximum storage drives of hundreds of terabytes. Again, that may be impressive, but it certainly is not exponential.

But while a paradigm shift might be needed in storage, which slows progress in the short term, that could mean little in the broader picture. As impressive as digital storage is, we know that compared to storing data as DNA – which can be presumed as a hypothetical limit – we have barely scratched the surface. While technology like that might not be on your laptop anytime soon, the potential is astonishing, with a single gram of human DNA able to store 215 petabytes (215 million gigabytes) of information. This is not the realm of abstract speculation, and humans have been able to store data as DNA since 2012, when Harvard University geneticists encoded a 52,000-word book using strands of DNA's four-letter alphabet of A, G, T, and C to encode the 0s and 1s of the digitised file.

While such progress might not have applications in the foreseeable future, here too discounting the possibility of going well beyond the final squares of the chessboard – in bandwidth and storage as well as processing speeds – appears unwise. It seems increasingly reasonable to presume that the primary constraints on technological advance are the laws of physics. For now, they remain a long way off.

The Power of Experience

Change doesn't have to be exponential to be transformative in the context of the Third Disruption. Around the same time Gordon Moore made his forecast about the future of computing, Bruce Henderson – founder of the Boston Consulting

Group – developed a concept that would come to be referred to as the Henderson Curve (more recently the Experience Curve). Based on observations he made while working with his clients, this soon became a sophisticated predictive model, outlining how the costs of a manufactured good decline by as much as 20 per cent every time capacity is doubled. The variables driving that behaviour are relatively simple, ranging from greater labour efficiency to improvements in product design. While the experience curve does not offer the same rapid transformation one sees in the exponential improvement of digital technologies, its dividend is of critical importance to extreme supply – specifically when it comes to renewable energy.

That's because the most important area where one sees the experience curve at work is with the price of photovoltaic (PV) cells, the main consumer technology for generating solar power. Here progress correlates almost perfectly to what Henderson would have predicted, with the cost of PV falling 20 per cent every time capacity has doubled over the last sixty years. When the technology was deployed for the first time aboard NASA's Vanguard 1 satellite in 1958, each panel was able to generate a maximum half a watt of energy at a cost of many thousands of dollars each. By the mid-1970s, that figure had fallen dramatically to $100 per watt, still uncompetitive with fossil fuels but impressive nonetheless. Yet by 2016 the price–performance ratio of solar had been transformed, with a watt of energy from a solar array costing as little as fifty cents, making it a genuine alternative to fossil fuels in countries with abundant sunshine.

Few disagree that this trend will continue, and with global solar capacity doubling every two years – it increased by a factor of one hundred between 2004 and 2014 – a virtuous cycle between increased capacity and ever-falling prices has been established. The critical question, as with Moore's Law, is how much longer that will continue.

What we know for certain is that, in principle, solar is more than capable of meeting the world's expanding energy needs. Given that the same amount of potential energy hits the Earth in ninety minutes as the whole of humanity consumes in a year then, even in the event of demand doubling over the coming decades, solar might not just be the greenest means of powering our world, but the cheapest one too.

Fortunately the same changes in the price–performance ratio of solar cells also apply to the mainstream technologies of renewable energy storage, lithium-ion batteries. There, recent falls in cost only serve to strengthen the conclusion that it is a question of when, rather than if, the world transitions to renewable energy.

From Crisis to Utopia

Ours is a finite world marked by constraints. To a large extent, these constraints define the five crises set to radically shape the course of the coming century.

Together, these crises – encompassing climate change, resource scarcity, ever-larger surplus populations, ageing and technological unemployment as a result of automation – are set to undermine capitalism's ability to reproduce itself. That is because they could dissolve some of its key features like the presumption of constant expansion and infinite resources, production for profit, and workers having to sell their labour.

In 1984 the futurist Stewart Brand made the now-iconic declaration 'Information wants to be free.' He would later clarify what that meant, saying,

On the one hand information wants to be expensive, because it's so valuable. The right information in the right place just changes your life. On the other hand, information wants to be free, because the cost of getting it out is getting lower and lower all the time. So you have these two fighting against each other.

As we shall see, information is the basis of value under modern capitalism – far more than we think. And yet technologies under that same economic system now paradoxically tend towards destroying the scarcity of information, and therefore its value.

It's unlikely Brand was aware of it in 1984, but Marx said something similar about the tendency of information towards extreme supply more than a century earlier:

Forces of production and social relations – two different sides of the development of the social individual – appear to capital as mere means, and are merely means for it to produce on its limited foundation. In fact, however, they are the material conditions to blow this foundation sky-high.

More than three decades after Brand stated his elegant observation we now know he was right – its plummeting cost shows information does want to be free. But by the middle of this century it will be increasingly clear that this also extends to labour, energy and resources too. This is the basis for a different set of social parameters underpinned by changes we can already observe around us: a world beyond jobs, profit and even scarcity.

3
What Is Fully Automated Luxury Communism?

The goal of the future is full unemployment, so we can play.

Arthur C. Clarke

Why FALC?

Why 'fully automated luxury communism'? Why those words and in that sequence? After all, many see communism as nothing more than a failed experiment of the twentieth century undeserving of our attention save learning from its mistakes. Some may admit that capitalism has numerous flaws, and may indeed end one day, but if communism is what comes next, that wouldn't be an improvement.

While it is true that a number of political projects have labelled themselves communist over the last century, the aspiration was neither accurate nor – as we will go on to see – technologically possible. 'Communism' is used here for the benefit of precision; the intention being to denote a society in which work is eliminated, scarcity replaced by abundance and where labour and leisure blend into one another. Given the possibilities arising from the Third Disruption, with the emergence of extreme supply in information, labour, energy and resources, it should be viewed not only as an idea adequate to our time but impossible before now. FALC does not underpin the trends of the Third Disruption – it is their conclusion.

If we want it.

Future Shock 1858

However people respond to the word 'communism', the word is associated with one person in particular – Karl Marx. It was he who claimed to see the contours of a new world at the precise moment industrial capitalism burned at its brightest.

That is not to say Marx was unique in thinking capitalism would end, nor that it would transition to something else. Indeed in this respect he was joined by, among others, two thinkers of the twentieth century, John Maynard Keynes and Peter Drucker, who despite being critics of his held similar views on how capitalism might lead to a system beyond it. By placing Marx alongside both thinkers, examining how each viewed the relationship of scarcity to capitalism and utopia, we can begin to create a clearer picture of what he meant by communism.

An aspect of Marx's thinking which remains underemphasised is how he recognised capitalism's tendency to progressively replace labour – animal and human, physical and cognitive – with machines. In a system replete with contradictions, it was this one in particular which rendered it a force of potential liberation. This is most clearly laid out in the 'Fragment on Machines', a short but important excerpt within the much larger *Grundrisse*. The reason you've likely never heard of either before, unlike the better-known *Communist Manifesto* or *Capital*, is that the *Grundrisse* was unpublished in German until 1939. Worse still, the text wasn't translated into English until 1973. As a result, its prescient observations exerted little influence over communist projects in the twentieth century.

That was a tragedy, because within the *Grundrisse* we not only encounter the first analysis of technological evolution under capitalism, but also the opportunities that creates. As Marx so memorably put it in the 'Fragment',

> Capital employs machinery, rather, only to the extent that it enables the worker to work a larger part of his time for capital, to relate to a larger part of his time as time which does not belong to him, to work longer for another. Through this process, the amount of labour necessary for the production of a given object is indeed reduced to a minimum, but only in order to realise a maximum of labour in the maximum number of such objects. The first aspect is important, because capital here – quite unintentionally – reduces human labour … to a minimum. This will redound to the benefit of emancipated labour, and is the condition of its emancipation.

Marx could not have been any clearer: competition compels capitalists to innovate in production. This leads to permanent experimentation with workflows and technologies, all in the pursuit of ever-greater efficiency. The logic of market demand means capitalists must produce goods and services as cheaply as they can, forcing them to constantly reduce overheads, in turn creating a never-ending cycle of automation, encompassing tasks and even whole jobs – substituting workers with machines. While generating huge amounts of suffering and exploitation under capitalism, under another system this represented a momentous opportunity.

In 1987 the US National Academy of Sciences published a report titled *Technology and Unemployment*. In it, restated almost word for word, is Marx's criticism of technological change under capitalism, the key difference being the report's authors consider such change to be wholly positive:

> Historically and, we believe, for the foreseeable future, reductions in labour requirements per unit of output resulting from new process technologies have been and will be outweighed by the beneficial employment effects of the expansion in total output that generally occurs.

So while production becomes ever more efficient, and leisure is valued as a social good, increased productivity doesn't lead to more free time but simply the production of more goods and services. In fairness to those defending it, such a view was not only founded on economic orthodoxy but also two centuries of observable change under capitalism. The difference with Marx in the *Grundrisse* is he thought there was an alternative, and that only in pursuing it could humans achieve freedom.

Communism: A World beyond Scarcity

While the average political commentator likes to cast Marx as an idealistic dreamer, the man himself repeatedly stated his distaste for describing what communism might actually look like – what he termed writing 'recipes for the cook-shops of the future'. While admirable in its humility, that is also irritating because one of the greatest minds to describe the shortcomings of the emerging system was well placed to at least suggest what might replace it. Marx's view, however, was that workers in struggle were uniquely positioned to arrive at concrete solutions.

He was certain about some features of the new society, however. One was that the arrival of communism would herald the end of any distinction between labour and leisure. More fundamentally, it would signal humanity's exit from what he called the 'realm of necessity' and entrance into the 'realm of freedom'.

But what did that mean? For Marx the realm of necessity was where we 'wrestle with nature to satisfy our wants and to maintain and reproduce life' – in other words it was a world defined by scarcity, something which had confronted us since the time of our hominid ancestors. In Marx's day it formed the central question of classical political economy: how do you efficiently and equitably allocate resources in a world where they are limited?

For Marx the realm of necessity was so far-reaching that it even included socialism. That was because, like capitalism, it had features such as work and scarcity – although as a system subject to democratic control these were rationalised and more socially just. While certainly preferable to capitalism, and something to be actively struggled for, socialism for Marx was a stepping stone to something else: communism and the realm of freedom.

This, by contrast, was marked not only by an absence of economic conflict and work but by a spontaneous abundance similar to the Golden Age of Hesiod or Telecleides, or the biblical Eden. Unlike in classical Greek poetry or religious scripture, however, for Marx this was a project to be aimed at rather than a legendary past to be revered. A realm of plenty beyond imagination wasn't something to recall or enjoy in the afterlife – it was a political project to aim for in the here and now. It was communism.

~

Despite the claim that Marx favoured violent revolution, the truth is he never believed the transition beyond capitalism would be an exclusively political process – something so simple to achieve as to merely require replacing one group of rulers with another. It certainly entailed class struggle and the working class gaining political power, but it also needed new ideas, technologies and social relations. Marx considered the working class to be the key to a future society, but only because its revolution was uniquely able to eliminate work and thereby end all class distinctions.

Thus despite repeated calls for the working class to liberate itself, Marx did not believe that work makes us free – nor that the society of work expands the scope of human possibility. To the contrary, his view was that communism was only possible when our labour – how we mix our cognitive and physical efforts with the world – becomes a route to self-development rather than a means of survival. Marx viewed this as contingent on technological change: the more developed the forces of production, the greater their capacity to offer a new kind of society where labour and leisure would blend into one:

> In a higher phase of communist society, after the enslaving subordination of the individual to the division of labour, and therewith also the antithesis between mental and physical labour, has vanished; after labour has become not only a means of life but life's prime want ... and all the springs of co-operative wealth flow more abundantly – only then can the narrow horizon of bourgeois right be crossed in its entirety and society inscribe on its banners: From each according to his ability, to each according to his needs!

With the arrival of communism any distinction between mental and physical labour would vanish, with work becoming more akin to play. This also meant a society with greater collective wealth, where all essential wants as well as creative desires are satisfied. Which is where luxury comes in. The concept, under conditions of scarcity, expresses that which is beyond utility, its essence an excess beyond the necessary. So as information, labour, energy and resources become permanently cheaper – and work and the limits of the old world are left behind – it turns out we don't just satisfy all of our needs, but dissolve any boundary between the useful and the beautiful. Communism is luxurious – or it isn't communism.

Post-Capitalism without Communism: J. M. Keynes

Marx was far from alone in claiming that capitalism creates the conditions for a society beyond it. Indeed, he was joined by the most influential economist of the twentieth century: John Maynard Keynes.

Keynes was by no means a radical, let alone a revolutionary. And yet in 1930, in the aftermath of the Wall Street crash and the start of what would become the Great Depression, he penned the most optimistic tract of his age, *Letter on the Economic Possibilities of Our Grandchildren*.

In this short, self-assured essay Keynes outlined a new society which he viewed as not only desirable, but inevitable. Like Marx in the *Grundrisse* he believed such a shift would prefigure a world unrecognisable from his own, yet also express its fullest development:

> I draw the conclusion that, assuming no important wars and no important increase in population, the economic problem may be solved, or be at least within sight of solution, within a hundred years. This means that the economic problem is not – if we look into the future – the permanent problem of the human race ... thus for the first time since his creation man will be faced with his real,

his permanent problem – how to use his freedom from pressing economic cares, how to occupy the leisure, which science and compound interest will have won for him, to live wisely and agreeably and well.

Keynes was an open critic of Marx despite also claiming to have never read him. And yet here one sees remarkable parallels between the two. For Marx, communism was a condition of abundance, a society where labour and leisure dissolved into each other, and where our natures were developed in a manner consistent with play. This was a world where scarcity – or as Keynes refers to it, 'the economic problem' – would finally be vanquished. In 1930 Keynes speculated about something remarkably similar and, amazingly, even had the confidence to put a date on it – foreseeing the arrival of post-scarcity as soon as 2030.

Other than Keynes's stated disdain for Marx's class-based politics in 'preferring the mud to the fish', what was it precisely that separated the two? The answer is the relationship between progress and politics. Unlike Marx, Keynes viewed capitalism as inevitably shifting to greater abundance, this resulting from its ability to become ever more productive over time while reducing the demand for labour. In *Economic Possibilities* his claim was that this would translate to a shorter working week, with improvements in productivity as technology progressed benefitting workers. In other words, leisure time was destined to increase while the need to work would slowly fade from view.

Marx, who likewise insisted on capitalism's ability to improve productivity, did not believe this benefitted anyone but the wealthy under the status quo, despite the possibility to do so. While Marx observed the same tendency to potential abundance, he viewed this as politically contested – with the spoils only going to the majority of society if they successfully fought for them in the struggle between classes.

The history of the twentieth century appeared to confirm that Keynes was right. In the five decades following 1927, despite the Great Depression, the real wages of unskilled workers in US manufacturing increased by 350 per cent, while pay for skilled labour increased by a factor of four. This, as we now know, was the golden age of capitalism, with productivity gains and high growth leading to rising wages and shorter working hours. Whether you were an employee or an industrialist, it was in your rational interest to protect the system.

This ended abruptly in the early 1970s, when wages decoupled from improvements to productivity – which now only fed the incomes of the very highest earners. This phenomenon extended beyond just the US. A 2014 report showed how real wage growth in Britain has been on a downward trend for forty years, with wages increasing an annual 2.9 per cent in the 1970s and 80s, 1.5 per cent in the 1990s, and 1.2 per cent in the 2000s. Since the 2008 crisis that incremental decline has gone into free-fall, with real household wages in Britain falling 10.4 per cent between 2007 and 2015, something entirely without precedent.

That already dire situation is only set to further deteriorate. After the release of the 2017 Autumn Budget, the Resolution Foundation, a London-based think tank, predicted that the 2010s would be the worst decade for UK wage growth since the late eighteenth century. In other words, Britain now faced a stagnation in living standards unseen since the rise of the Second Disruption. While Keynes was right to note the possibility of capitalism creating such abundance as to potentially nurture a system beyond it, he predicted none of this.

That is because he did not think his vision of a society beyond capitalism — of high productivity, automation and leisure — was internally contradictory. So where Marx saw an intractable problem, between a system based on work and market rationing on one side and abundance on the other, Keynes saw an easy procession from one world to the next.

With each passing day, particularly since the 2008 crisis, it seems ever more obvious that Marx was right. The five crises of this century are either an existential threat to humanity, or the birth pangs of something better.

Despite what Keynes predicted, neither is inevitable.

Post-Capitalism and Information: Peter Drucker

Unlike Marx and Keynes, Peter Drucker was not a political economist but a theorist of management. Like them, however, he believed that capitalism was a contingent, finite system with a distinct endpoint. He called that endpoint 'post-capitalism' and, as in the thinking of Marx and Keynes, it represented the full development of modernity.

At virtually the same time that HTML was publicly released, Drucker identified how information had become the primary factor of production — more so than the historic trio of labour, land and capital. As he wrote in 1993, 'that knowledge has become the resource rather than a resource, is what makes our society post-capitalist ... it creates new social dynamics. It creates new economic dynamics. It creates new politics.'

Drucker believed that society went through such rearrangements regularly, with Western history showing a 'sharp transformation' every several hundred years. All of which meant that within a few short decades, 'society re-arranges itself — its world view; its basic values; its social and political infrastructure; its arts; its key institutions. Fifty years later there is a new world'. Drucker believed the shift to post-capitalism to be one such transformation.

In Drucker's periodisation of history, disruptions are viewed as happening more regularly than understood here, with the implications of each being less far-reaching. Nevertheless, his view of historic change, where the material relations of society inflect ideas and social reality, undeniably resembles that of Marx. Below are Marx's words, written in the mid-nineteenth century. They could just as easily have been uttered by Drucker in the early 1990s.

> At a certain stage of development, the material productive forces of society come into conflict with the existing relations of production ... then begins an era of social revolution. The changes in the economic foundation lead sooner or later to the transformation of the whole immense superstructure.

Taylorism and the Productivity Revolution

For Drucker, knowledge and its application changed significantly with the arrival of the Industrial Revolution and capitalism, after which it went from being a private good to a public one, something applied to doing rather than being. With Watt's steam engine and the new society it fostered, the meaning and the purpose of knowledge fundamentally changed. As it was applied to tools, processes and products, the notion of technology as a distinct field began to emerge. By the 1870s it was this relationship between knowledge and technology which drove what Drucker labelled the 'Productivity Revolution'.

The father of this revolution was Frederick Taylor, an American mechanical engineer and pioneer in scientific management. Until Taylor, whose professional life took off in the 1880s, the scientific method had never been applied to the study of work in order to maximise output. Yet within a few short decades this became a dogma – massively expanding productivity and improving the standard of living for the average worker. After the rise of 'Taylorism', at least according to Drucker, value became more about the continued refinement and application of information than about labour, land or capital.

Once again similarities between Drucker's thinking on the matter and that of his predecessors, particularly Marx, are clear. As Marx would write in the *Grundrisse*,

> But to the degree that large industry develops, the creation of real wealth comes to depend less on labour time and on the amount of labour employed than on the power of the agencies set in motion during labour time, whose 'powerful effectiveness' ... depends rather on the general state of science and on the progress of technology, or the application of this science to production.

Remarkably, Marx even adds how this undermines labour as the central factor of production:

> No longer does the worker insert a modified natural thing as middle link between the object and himself; rather, he inserts the process of nature, transformed into an industrial process, as a means between himself and inorganic nature, mastering it. He steps to the side of the production process instead of being its chief actor.

Just like Drucker, Marx believed that this tension, between knowledge becoming a central factor of production and an economic system built on labour, inevitably meant a transition. Only for him the result was inexorable conflict, with the new only able to substitute for the old as the result of class struggle. According to Marx, even with the most developed machinery the worker could well be forced to 'work longer than the savage does, or than he himself did with the simplest, crudest tools'. Technology transformed work, and could improve people's lives, but only if it was coupled with an appropriate politics.

For Drucker, however, the transformation didn't stop with Taylor. He observed an increasingly central role for knowledge as capitalism changed over the twentieth century. Thus, while the period after the 1880s saw a productivity revolution, and the decades following 1945 a 'management revolution', it was in the 'information revolution' that he saw production increasingly based on the 'application of knowledge to knowledge'. While knowledge had always been important – after all, the essence of the First Disruption resided in mastering the information content of crops and animals through selective breeding – with the rise of digitisation and information technology, Drucker viewed this process as reaching some kind of end point, with labour, land and capital critically sidelined as factors of production.

In Marx, Keynes and Drucker, we are offered three futures, each articulating a society beyond capitalism only made possible by its fullest development. While it seemed otherwise for much of the last century, it now appears that in regard to declining living standards, regardless of productivity improvements, Marx was right, and Keynes wrong. Technological change can potentially lead us to abundance, as Keynes so bravely predicted in 1930, but only if it is accompanied by a politics that demands as much. And Drucker? What he correctly grasped was where value was increasingly located – in information.

But what none of the three clearly outlined is precisely

how this new mode of production would stitch itself into the fabric of the present. Remarkably the person who did – almost without knowing it – would later become the chief economist for the World Bank. His name is Paul Romer.

Information Goods Want to Be Free – Really

In 1990, at just 35, Romer authored a now celebrated academic paper titled *Endogenous Technological Change*. There he effectively crystallised what Drucker would write just a few years later, highlighting the new and critical importance of knowledge to economic growth.

Understanding what correlates with growth had long been an obsession for economists, principally because by assessing growth's co-factors you could infer what caused it – savings rates, population growth, rising wages – and reverse-engineer a recipe for prosperity. Prior to Romer's paper, technological change was presumed to be 'exogenous', an external, constant variable akin to background noise and, therefore, unimportant. But Romer disagreed, claiming that given market forces themselves drive innovation, technological change should be understood as a major driver of capitalist development. The question was how this functioned and with what consequences.

Romer defined technological change as 'an improvement in the instructions for mixing together raw materials'. Technological change was therefore, perhaps counter-intuitively, immaterial – amounting to nothing more than an upgraded re-arrangement of previous information. 'Instructions for working with raw materials are inherently different from other economic goods,' Romer concluded. So over time, as technology develops, the value increasingly arises from the instructions for materials as opposed to the materials themselves.

There was only one problem. What was now identified as the most valuable aspect of a commodity was also – technically, at least – capable of infinite replication at near zero cost: 'once the cost of creating a new set of instructions has been incurred the instructions can be used over and over again at no additional cost. Developing new and better instructions is equivalent to incurring a fixed cost.' Romer made no mention of the hacker movement, but this was starting to sound remarkably similar to Stewart Brand's conclusion that 'information wants to be free' some six years earlier.

This contradiction was particularly portentous for market capitalism. As Larry Summers and J. Bradford DeLong would write in August 2001, just a month after the file-sharing service Napster was taken down, 'the most basic condition for economic efficiency … [is] that price equal marginal cost.' They went on: 'with information goods, the social and marginal cost of distribution is close to zero.' This held true not only for films, music, books and academic papers but also for the design of an industrial robot or pharmaceutical drug. Indeed, as subsequent chapters will make clear, it holds true for ever broader swathes of the economy. Therein lies the paradox for capitalism, a system under which things are produced for exchange and profit.

> If information goods are to be distributed at their marginal cost of production – zero – they cannot be created and produced by entrepreneurial firms that use revenues obtained from sales to consumers to cover their costs. If information goods are to be created and produced … (companies) must be able to anticipate selling their products at a profit to someone.

Remarkably, two of the most esteemed economists in the world were conceding a quite remarkable truth: the price mechanism had broken down for what should be the most valuable part of the commodity – its instructions. Economics, for so long obsessed with the issue of dealing with scarcity, began to see glimpses of something beyond it – the only problem being this broke down the system of incentives by which people are meant to create things under capitalism, namely profit.

Their proposed solution – of exclusion and creating artificial scarcity – was sketchy but revealing. This would be achieved through creating closed voluntary architectures (as Apple would later pursue with their products for example), changes to copyright law and the active promotion of monopolies – something previously viewed as being at odds with functioning, healthy markets. Summers and DeLong even conceded such a point when they wrote that

> temporary monopoly power and profits are the reward needed to spur private enterprise … the right way to think about this complex set of issues is not clear, but it is clear that the competitive paradigm cannot be fully appropriate … we do not yet know what the right replacement paradigm will be.

Nearly two decades later and still nobody can answer that question.

Until now.

II.
New Travellers

There is only one condition in which we can imagine managers not needing subordinates, and masters not needing slaves. This condition would be that each instrument could do its own work, at the word of command or by intelligent anticipation, like the statues of Daedalus or the tripods made by Hephaestus, of which Homer relates that 'Of their own motion they entered the conclave of Gods on Olympus', as if a shuttle should weave of itself, and a plectrum should do its own harp playing.

Aristotle

4

Full Automation: Post-Scarcity in Labour

Productivity is for robots.

Kevin Kelly

When Capital Becomes Labour

In 2011 the *Economist*, in circulation since 1843, posed its readers a question: 'What happens when ... machines are smart enough to become workers? In other words, when capital becomes labour?'

While early giants of classical political economy, such as Adam Smith and David Ricardo, did not view capitalist society as defined by conflict between classes, they did presume that labour would always remain distinct from 'capital stock', and that workers could never equate to human-made goods used in production such as machinery, tools and buildings.

Yet nearly 250 years after Smith wrote *The Wealth of Nations*, the publication most committed to defending his legacy was now uncertain whether one of the central premises of his thinking would endure for much longer. Such doubt resides at the very heart of what the Third Disruption means. If capital can become labour – if tools produced by humans can subsequently perform any task they themselves complete – then, within a market system, the price a worker can demand for their time collapses.

Such an outcome would bring a number of problems, the most immediate being underconsumption. This is a problem whose relationship to automation is best expressed in a meeting recounted in the *Economist* article, alleged to have taken place in the 1950s between Henry Ford II and Walter Reuther, leader of the United Auto Workers union. Ford had invited Reuther to examine one of the company's newly built factories, and as the two began to walk across the shop floor he is said to have pointed at some newly acquired industrial robots, inquiring how such machines would pay their dues to the union. Reuther's response is reputed to have been immediate: 'Henry, how are you going to get them to buy your cars?'

This conversation between Ford and Reuther, whether it actually took place or not, demonstrates a paradox central to the future of capitalism. While wanting to all but eliminate workers from production in order to save money, Ford also wanted to maintain demand for the company's products, now made more efficiently than ever. Simply put, Ford wanted cheap employees but affluent consumers – something which simply wasn't possible.

His grandfather, the first Henry Ford, knew better. In 1914 he had shocked the industry by announcing that company employees would see their pay doubled to as much as $5 a day. Behind that decision was the pressing issue of high employee turnover, with Ford viewing decisive action as necessary given the large costs of constantly training new workers.

Many contemporaries claimed the $5 figure – unrivalled anywhere else – was simply a publicity stunt, while others said it betokened a unique perception on the behalf of the Ford Company: higher wages weren't only needed to retain staff, but also to ensure the people making the cars could also afford to buy them.

It was to be that second interpretation which made more sense over time. Today it seems undeniable that Ford intuited how industries based on mass consumption, like the embryonic car industry, require ordinary people to enjoy leisure as much they endure work. That would explain why Ford also supported the eight-hour day and the five-day week, writing of the latter, in 1926, 'It is high time to rid ourselves of the notion that leisure for workmen is either lost time or a class privilege.'

Those words drove at the heart of how twentieth-century capitalism came to view itself: functioning properly, the system allowed employees to buy the goods and services their work had created. This proved the basis for a compromise across classes built on rising productivity, profits for the wealthy and progressively improving living standards for everyone else.

For a long time things seemed to go to plan, with improvements in productivity feeding through to higher wages and an increasingly widespread abundance. As a result Reuther's response appeared unduly pessimistic – the conclusion of someone with a political bias against the consequences of technological change. And yet today, as the *Economist*'s rhetorical challenge makes clear, it is one of the key questions shaping our future. Nobody, so far at least, has a definitive answer.

Peak Horse

The First Disruption started around 10,000 BC as *Homo sapiens,* likely somewhere between the Mediterranean Sea and Persian Gulf, began building a world of agriculture, settlement and surplus. Rather than relying on the power of their own bodies, humans started to draw on domesticated animals, while increasingly complex forms of society permitted slavery, hierarchy and the emergence of early energy technologies. Beneath this promethean change, however, the critical disruptor was our new mastery over biological life, this arising from recent knowledge about how to breed for specific traits and reprogramme elements of the natural environment. In its own way, this was a revolution in information, although we wouldn't know its underlying mechanisms until the mid-nineteenth century.

After the First Disruption physical work was increasingly performed by novel configurations of human labour, animals and the elements, and by the twelfth century the sight of the water and windmill was increasingly common across much of Europe. This was a world where motive force was overwhelmingly organic: oxen in the field, horses to travel, human motion for the spinning wheel, even a special breed of canine – the Turnspit dog – would turn meat while it roasted.

In a world absent of concentrated forms of energy, or significant mechanical power, change was slow, with political tumult or economic downturn often spelling technological reverse. Most Europeans would not drink water as clean as that found in Ancient Rome until the twentieth century, with no city achieving its scale and prominence until London in the early 1800s.

That was the case until the emergence of the Second Disruption, which presented itself not only as a new paradigm in labour and production, but also energy. Now fossil fuels – plentiful, powerful and reliable – would replace the brawn of human and beast, in a matter of decades transforming the world. Like any great transition, such change had its own victims and they extended far beyond the Turnspit dog. Furthermore, the line between crisis and opportunity was not always clear, and as features of the new world scraped against the certainties of the old, it was easy to confuse progress for decay.

An outstanding example of this can be found in London in the final years of the nineteenth century. By 1894 the British capital, now the largest city on Earth, confronted a crisis of epic proportions. Having survived the threat of invasion for almost a millennium, be it the Spanish Armada or Napoleon's Revolutionary Army, an unexpected foe now imperilled the city – horse shit. The 'Horse Manure Crisis', as it was termed by *The Times* that year, struck fear into the hearts of Londoners who soon expected their city to be so covered in faeces that its streets would resemble the canals of Venice.

Such a threat had been a long time in the making. Over the preceding century London's population had quadrupled, and it had no rival in industry, social complexity or geographical spread, with New York only surpassing it on each measure by the early 1920s.

This success was what precipitated the 1894 crisis. London was at the leading edge of trends resulting from the Second Disruption, especially rapid population growth – as fewer infants and children died and life expectancy, after a generation, began to increase. This, combined with rapid urbanisation, began to create major infrastructural problems in housing, transport and sanitation.

But while the Second Disruption meant more people, more trade and more work, a vital piece of technology remained from the pre-steam era: the horse. Even as late as the 1890s – when some of London's streets had electric lights – there were around 11,000 hansom cabs in the city, as well as several thousand horse-drawn buses, each employing twelve large animals. That meant a staggering 50,000 horses transporting people around the city every day, not to mention the many more horse-drawn carts and drays delivering goods. The sheer number of animals, in addition to their size, meant London's streets were covered by at least 1.5 million pounds of horse manure every day.

Which is why when *The Times* speculated in 1894 about the city a half century thereafter it concluded, 'In fifty years, every street in London will be buried under nine feet of manure.' Such a conclusion seemed reasonable – after all, cities of this kind had never existed before and they appeared to be unsustainable. Even an urban studies conference convened specifically to discuss the issue some four years later, failed to arrive at any solutions.

And yet we now know such predictions never came to pass. The technologies of the internal combustion engine and electricity, already in evidence as *The Times* penned its obituary for the world's leading experiment in urban living, meant cars, buses and electric trams replaced the horse-drawn cart and carriage. By 1912, a seemingly insurmountable problem had been solved. In every major city horses were being replaced with motorised vehicles. What looked like a secular problem was merely a hangover of the First Disruption coming up against the birth pangs of the Second.

Peak Human

While the Second Disruption began to unfold in the last decades of the eighteenth century, the date of *The Times* prognostication – 1894 – makes clear just how long it took for many of its innovations to permeate across society.

So while the motive power of animals, in this case horses, characterised the technology and energy model of another age, the most advanced economies wouldn't reach 'peak horse' until the early twentieth century. The United States, which by that time had become the world's largest and most advanced economy, wouldn't reach its apogee until 1915 when over 26 million horses lived and worked alongside humans. Within just a few decades, however, they would disappear from the world of work, substituted in a range of tasks by machines which were more reliable, didn't get sick and, most importantly, led to far greater productivity. Paradoxical as it might seem, we employed animals like never before at the very moment they were becoming obsolete.

This was a theme returned to in 1983 by the Nobel Prize–winning economist Wassily Leontief. For Leontief, human labour in the twenty-first century would come to resemble horses at the turn of the twentieth. Now, as then, a key source of value-creation and wealth would become obsolete:

> Computers and robots [will] replace humans in the exercise of mental functions in the same way as mechanical power replaced them in the performance of physical tasks. As time goes on, more and more complex mental functions will be performed by machines ... this means that the role of humans as the most important factor of production is bound to diminish—in the same way that the role of horses in agricultural production was first diminished and then eliminated by the introduction of tractors.

If Leontief is right, then many of the problems we presently view as intractable may, within a few short decades, seem as outlandish to the next generation as London sinking in excrement does to us.

~

The evidence appears to lend at least some weight to Leontief's conclusion, nowhere more so than in manufacturing. In 1970 there were around 1,000 industrial robots worldwide. By the beginning of 2016 that number had risen to 1.8 million and is expected to exceed 3 million by 2020. Since 2010 the global stock of industrial robots has increased by an annual average of more than 10 per cent. Compound growth means if that trend persists manufacturing won't just stop creating jobs – as it already has done despite massively increased output – but their numbers will significantly decline.

The ever-greater employment of industrial robots correlates entirely with what can be observed in both manufacturing jobs and output. In the two decades following Leontief's prediction, information technology and robotics allowed the US steel industry to increase output from 75 to 125 million tonnes while the number of workers declined from 289,000 to 74,000. More broadly, the US lost 2 million manufacturing jobs over the period to automation – around 11 per cent of the sector.

Between 1997 and 2005 that trend only continued to accelerate with US manufacturing output increasing by another 60 per cent while almost 4 million more jobs in the sector disappeared. The explanation why is straightforward: a major rise in productivity allowed industry to produce more with less. By 2007 American manufacturers were using more than six times as much equipment, including computers and software, as they had done twenty years earlier – while doubling the amount of capital used per hour of employee work. Contrary to popular misconceptions in the US of millions of manufacturing jobs being lost to cheaper workers abroad, for the most part they have simply been automated – subject to ever improving efficiency.

Surprisingly, less developed economies fare even worse over the same period, with Brazil enduring a 20 per cent decline in industrial employment and Japan 16 per cent. Perhaps most impressive of all is China which, in the process of becoming the world's leading manufacturer, lost 16 million industrial jobs. As one journal observed, 'though it is of course easy to demonstrate that plenty of industrial production still takes place, and that this is not only in important exporter nations such as China, the share of workers actually employed in manufacture has now been declining for almost two decades at the global level.'

The extent of such change is most obvious in those countries which industrialised first, and today Britain and the United States have a smaller percentage of their workforce in manufacturing than they did in the early years of their respective industrial revolutions. Because this process of productivity gains leading to job losses in manufacturing is global, some forecasts predict that at the current rate of displacement, factory employment, which accounted for 163 million jobs in 2003, is likely to employ no more than a few million people by 2040.

Manufacturing work, while often more complex than many imagine, is repetitive and thus highly liable to automation. As we approach 'peak human' it is in this sector where – just as with horses in the opening decades of the twentieth century – the old world will transition to the new more quickly than many imagine.

A stunning representation of the changes automation can effect on productivity and jobs can be seen with the Dutch tech giant Philips, one of the world's leading companies in the manufacture of lighting. While the business has more than a hundred facilities located across multiple continents, their Drachten plant in the Netherlands is home to some of the most sophisticated industrial technology on Earth. Here,

128 robot arms do the same work as hundreds of employees in the company's factory in Zhuhai, China. Philips claim that productivity is ten times higher in their Drachten plant, with the robotic arms so quick they are kept behind glass screens to ensure the safety of the few employees that remain.

Such hugely differing levels of productivity, combined with worker's wages in China rising continuously for two decades, means automation is beginning to put pressure on those industries which relocated to the Global South after the 1970s. While many jobs in manufacturing remain there for now, lower levels of comparative development will count for little. Indeed it is estimated that China will be spending nearly $60 billion a year on robotics by 2020.

In 2012 Terry Gou, CEO of Foxconn, compared his company's 1 million employees to animals and complained that managing them 'gives me a headache'. That partly explains why, just three years later, a single Foxconn factory in Kunshan, China, substituted robots for sixty thousand employees. Ultimately, countries in the Global South are no more immune to the pressures of automation in industry and manufacturing than those of Europe and North America. And while countries like China and South Korea benefitted from the global relocation of production after the 1970s, the same will not hold true for today's lower GDP countries like Bangladesh and Indonesia. This time, capital's 'fix' is primarily technological rather than spatial. That has stark implications for how poorer countries might navigate development.

The End of Mass Agriculture

While it feels like manufacturing is in uncharted waters thanks to technological unemployment, we've been here before. Indeed what the Third Disruption is presently doing to manufacturing mirrors what the Second Disruption did to the breakthrough technology of humanity: agriculture.

Agriculture, as already outlined, was the innovation at the heart of the First Disruption, allowing surplus and ever more complex forms of cooperation to transform what it meant to be human. And while one can argue about distinct technological periods within even that – as Peter Drucker and Jeremy Rifkin do – even as recently as the nineteenth century, 60 per cent of the population in countries like Italy and France worked in agriculture. Whether it was the Roman Empire of the first century AD, Europe during Charlemagne or Eastern China under the Song Dynasty a millennium ago, the average person worked in farming, almost always cultivating land which wasn't theirs.

Today things look rather different. Just 4 per cent of Italy's labour market is in agriculture, while the figure is less than 3 per cent for France, 2 per cent in the UK and 1 per cent in the United States – a nation which leads the world in the production of milk, corn, chicken and beef.

In short, we feed more people more food than ever before with ever fewer people doing the work. While that might sound trivial, as recently as a century ago it would have struck most as entirely implausible.

Similarly, by the beginning of the twenty-first century it was readily apparent that industries central to the Second Disruption – such as iron and steel production, as well as the manufacture of consumer durables like cars and electronic goods – required ever fewer workers to produce ever more output. This trend, an effect of rising productivity, is now observable on a global scale. Even in China, by far the world's largest exporter of goods, less than a quarter of the labour market works in industry.

The default presumption among economists, at least until

recently, was that just as many people's work shifted from agriculture to industry something similar would unfold with services. Post-industrial service-based economies would replace those built on manufacturing. To some extent, this was borne out: even China's service sector grew relative to manufacturing while it became the world's leading industrial power. In countries like France, Britain and the United States services now comprise 80 per cent of both economic output and jobs.

There is only one problem with the presumption that services, high- or low-skilled, will provide jobs where industry and agriculture no longer will. It turns out that any repetitive endeavour – whatever the industry – can be automated within the context of rising digitisation. Just as we reached 'peak horse' a century ago, as one paradigm came up against another, within a generation we are set for peak human.

Rise of the Robots

In 1997 IBM's Deep Blue defeated grandmaster Garry Kasparov over a series of chess matches, becoming the first computer to do so. While that was an iconic moment in the unfolding story of humans and machines, it paled in comparison to Watson, also built by IBM, when it later defeated Ken Jennings and Brad Rutter – two of the greatest *Jeopardy!* players in the history of the TV quiz show. Chess is a uniquely challenging game, but *Jeopardy!*, which demands real-time pattern recognition and creative thinking, more closely resembles the features associated with distinctively human intelligence.

Not long after, Ken Jennings neatly summed up what that defeat might mean for white-collar work – which values pattern recognition and creative thinking – over the coming decades.

Just as factory jobs were eliminated in the twentieth century by new assembly-line robots, Brad and I were the first knowledge-industry workers put out of work by the new generation of 'thinking' machines. 'Quiz show contestant' may be the first job made redundant by Watson, but I'm sure it won't be the last.

That was an insightful conclusion. While machines had bested humans at things like chess and solving maths problems – feats we typically associate with genius – they did so by brute force, completing incomprehensible numbers of calculations. Deep Blue assessed 200 million chess positions per second – a colossal number made possible by riding the wave of Moore's Law and exponential progress. Those trends have only continued, meaning that today you can download a chess engine programme like Houdini 6 for your home computer and it would beat Deep Blue almost every time.

And yet a paradox has emerged. It has become clear that more 'processor power' is actually required for managing what we have historically considered to be low-level tasks for humans, such as motor-sensory coupling, spatial awareness and unanticipated responses. In other words, it is harder to build a machine that can wash the dishes than one that can solve complex mathematical problems. This contradiction is known as Moravec's Paradox, after the technologist who defined it. From the perspective of technological unemployment it was a hugely important observation, showing how even 'low-skilled' jobs, from construction to fruit picking, could remain immune from automation. Even as machines beat chess grandmasters and former supercomputers found their processing power equalled by $400 games consoles, they could barely walk up a flight of stairs.

For a while this paradox appeared intractable. Even at the turn of the twenty-first century, some fifty years after the

Third Disruption began, the possibility of a machine with even the balance and coordination of a small child seemed remote.

But then the impossible suddenly became inevitable. Enter Atlas, the robot who learned to somersault.

Atlas Somersaults

If you go to YouTube and type 'PETMAN prototype' into the search bar, the first video that appears, posted in October 2009, is a demonstration of a biped robot developed by Massachusetts-based company Boston Dynamics. Awkward and attached to several cables, PETMAN looks like the love-child of a subwoofer and Bambi on ice.

Now type in 'What's new, Atlas?' On your screen will appear a video of another robot manufactured by the same company. Only this video was published in late 2017 and the robot isn't just walking without cables, it's doing box jumps and backflips. It doesn't end there; elsewhere on the company's YouTube channel you can see videos of Atlas jogging outside or doing 'parkour' as it jumps three successive steps of forty centimetres each without breaking stride. This would appear to indicate that Moravec's paradox is close to being overcome, with machines able to match humans in fine dexterity and spatial awareness sooner than we think. The descendants of Atlas another nine years from now may plausibly have the kind of coordination typically associated with an ice skater, gymnast or sculptor.

The reason why is simple: the progress from PETMAN to Atlas is underpinned by the improvements outlined in the second chapter, as we see exponential gains in the price–performance ratio of digital technologies, from cameras and sensors to chips, and the experience curve in areas such as energy storage. A case in point: until 2015 Atlas had to be permanently plugged into a wall socket. Now, with its 3.7-kilowatt-hour lithium-ion battery pack, it can walk around for about an hour. These trends are only set to continue.

But while robots whose movements authentically resemble those of humans aren't quite here yet, another category of machine – drawing on the same gains in digitisation and the dividend of exponential progress – is on the verge of transforming whole industries. It is the leading edge of a transformation which will mean not only the loss of countless jobs, but entire professions. And just like the acrobatics of Atlas, nobody saw it coming – until it was right in front of them.

Autonomous Vehicles

In 2002 the American defence agency DARPA announced a 'Grand Challenge' for driverless cars scheduled to take place in the Mojave Desert in spring 2004. The proposed route was two hundred and forty kilometres long and the prize, for whichever car finished first, was set at $1 million.

While some of the most brilliant minds in America applied themselves to the task, not one of the fifteen teams present at the start line was able to complete the course. The 'winner', built by Carnegie Mellon University, was only able to successfully navigate 5 per cent of the route. While the challenge had been ambitious – after all, the point was to stretch the entrants' abilities – few thought it would descend into such farce. One observer even labelled the episode 'the debacle in the desert'. To any reasonable person the possibility of autonomous vehicles seemed decades away.

And yet, just six years later in 2010, Google announced their self-driving cars had 'logged in over 140,000 miles' with seven test vehicles completing over 1,000 miles each without any human intervention – including difficult terrain like San Francisco's notoriously steep Lombard Street. Since then the likes of Apple, Tesla and Uber have entered the game, not to mention the older incumbents of the automobile industry. By 2016 Uber's then-CEO Travis Kalanick was clear about the importance of self-driving vehicles for any transport company: 'It starts with understanding that the world is going to go self-driving and autonomous ... what would happen if we weren't a part of that future? If we weren't part of the autonomy thing? Then the future passes us by.' In the span of just eleven years the technology underpinning autonomous vehicles had improved so dramatically that they went from a totem of public ridicule to influencing the business models of some of the world's most valuable companies.

That is how exponential technologies work: ponderously at first, and then a sudden transformation – a tendency historically visible with personal computing, smartphones, the internet and soon the descendants of Atlas. For now, however, the technology that will turn self-driving cars from engineering possibility to background feature in our everyday lives remains to be perfected.

Importantly, the way this challenge is being approached by the likes of Google and Uber offers an insight into how automation may diffuse across other parts of the economy and eliminate jobs. The strategy runs something like this: begin by acquiring massive amounts of data to allow algorithms to model and reproduce outcomes and work their way through highly repetitive tasks. After that, incorporate machine learning which is able to respond to unexpected situations arising beyond the data viewed as otherwise typical. Combining these steps yields something which can perform a wide range of jobs – from complex surgery to picking fruit and even writing journalism.

Such an approach is feasible because processor power is constantly improving and data sets are getting larger every second. But the nature of jobs under capitalism – comprised of tasks rather than the generalist approach seen with artisanal labour – also plays a part. Industrial change, particularly since the 1880s, has meant each job is reduced to a managed set of components, all of which are measured and managed as scientifically as possible. Without knowing it, the project of Frederick Taylor and his productivity revolution – for Drucker the first step in making information the primary factor of production – has turned out to be just as crucial to peak human as the exponential progress of digital technologies.

Autonomous vehicles offer an instructive example. To create cars that drive themselves, the likes of Uber, Tesla and Google didn't model and then replicate how humans drive – this remains well beyond our present technology. Rather, they tried to solve the problem by breaking it down into a set of component operations and putting a data processing system on wheels. As a result these vehicles can navigate streets and motorways by relying on precise GPS data, huge amounts of information regarding maps, and a continuous stream of real-time updates on other cars, potential obstacles, pedestrians and all the variables human drivers have to consider. All of this is achieved with a myriad of sensors, lasers and cameras processing information as 1s and 0s.

Even in isolation the arrival of autonomous vehicles likely spells the disappearance of whole professions. In 2014, driving accounted for around 4 million jobs in the US alone, and according to a report by Goldman Sachs the country could see job losses at a rate of 300,000 a year as autonomous vehicles become an integrated feature of modern society. From the perspective of business that would be entirely understandable: logistics vehicles running twenty-four hours a day, seven days a week, offer massive savings. And while there is a temptation to say machines can't be liable for accidents, with over 1.3 million annual road deaths worldwide, and 40,000 in the US alone, it won't be long before the technology is sufficiently advanced that such an argument could be reversed. That's before mentioning taxis, buses, trains, planes and warehousing. All of these industries will be impacted in a similar way, if at varying paces, and near-entirely automated in little more than a generation.

Technological Unemployment Is Coming

A 2015 study by the Bank of England isolated how technological change, in particular the rise of machine learning, would mean the loss of 15 million jobs in the UK – 40 per cent of the labour market – over the next few decades. Underpinning that would be the shrinking space for uniquely human skills, with this limiting any chance for workers to up-skill in response. A year later, the bank's governor, Mark Carney, repeated those forecasts saying many livelihoods could be 'mercilessly destroyed' by technological change, and that ever-higher income inequality could be one of the major consequences.

Those findings confirmed the conclusions of an earlier report published by two Oxford University academics, Carl Benedikt Frey and Michael Osborne. In 2013 they claimed that 47 per cent of all US jobs were at 'high risk' of being automated, with a further 19 per cent facing medium risk. Elsewhere Peter Sondergaard, research director for the consultancy Gartner, predicted that by 2025 one in three jobs will be automated as the result of an emerging 'super class' of technologies, with general purpose robotics and machine learning leading the way. Finally, in a 2016 report to Congress, White House economists forecast an 83 per cent chance that workers earning less than $20 per hour will lose their jobs to robots in the medium term.

The Bank of England, Oxford University, a global technology consultancy and the United States Congress are far from siren voices that are easy to dismiss. This is the heart of the economics and business establishment. While not everyone agrees on the extent to which technology will create unemployment in the short term, even more conservative voices think unavoidable change is not far away.

Take the Millennium Project. Launched in the 1990s by several UN organisations, it expects global unemployment to increase to 16 per cent by 2030 before rising to 24 per cent by the middle of the century. While that is more guarded than the Bank of England's predictions, or the claims of Peter Sondergaard, such a shift would more than test business as usual. A world of 10 billion people facing the challenges of climate change, ageing and resource shortages would endure levels of joblessness similar to those confronting Greece today – a country where 50 per cent youth unemployment has given rise to the most polarised society in Europe. Not only would such a scenario generate political and social turbulence on a global scale but importantly – and unlike with Greece – there would be no promise of a brighter tomorrow, however far away.

The most frequent rejoinder to all of this is that while the jobs of today may well disappear, others will emerge in their place. After all, that is what has always happened in the past. And yet that isn't quite true. Eighty per cent of today's professions existed a century ago, with the number of people employed in the 20 per cent of new occupations comprising only one in ten jobs. While the world economy may be much bigger now than it was in 1900, employing more people and enjoying far higher output per person, the lines of work nearly everyone performs – drivers, nurses, teachers and cashiers – aren't particularly new.

Actually Existing Automation

In March 2017 Amazon launched its Amazon GO store in downtown Seattle. Using computer vision, deep learning algorithms, and sensor fusion to identify selected items the company looked to build a near fully automated store without cashiers. Here Amazon customers would be able to buy items simply by swiping in with a phone, choosing the things they wanted and swiping out to leave, their purchases automatically debited to their Amazon account.

Several months later Amazon acquired Whole Foods Market for $13.7 billion. While that might have appeared a strange acquisition for a company whose core business is online retail, the purchase provided them with the supply chain capabilities to support Amazon GO and take aim at the $800 billion global grocery market.

Company management plans to use six people per shift in each Amazon Go store compared to the seventy-two employees found in the average US supermarket. When you consider the labour costs as well as Amazon's singular advantage in high automation warehousing – here too they are a world leader with their 'KIVA' robot – it quickly becomes clear the company could come to dominate areas of offline retail just as they presently do online. That is, except in China, where in late 2017 the local retailer JD.com announced the opening of hundreds of 'unmanned stores' ahead of anyone else.

Regardless whether it is Amazon or a rival who gains first-mover advantage, the trends are clear. The future of retail, as with logistics and warehousing, is automated. Yes, some jobs will remain, but when you consider that salesperson and cashier are the two leading jobs in the United States – and indeed most other countries – the prospect is a frightening one. Some might say customers want an emotional connection when they shop, and in certain contexts that may well be true, but most of the time the primary consideration will be the best product at the most affordable price. That will mean cutting labour costs wherever possible.

Rather than distant challenges, the retail industry now anticipates major layoffs in the area. Before Amazon Go was even announced, the British Retail Consortium predicted almost a third of the country's 3 million retail jobs would disappear by 2025, resulting in 900,000 lost jobs as companies turn to technology to replace workers.

As with self-driving cars and Atlas, all of this is possible because of extreme supply in information – from things like image and range sensors, to stereo cameras, deep learning algorithms, and the ubiquity of smartphones and online accounts. The same holds true elsewhere in the supply chain, from the warehousing robots using sensors and barcodes controlled by a central server, to the autonomous vehicles set to oversee distribution and delivery – whether by vehicle or drone.

But even among those who accept that common jobs like warehousing, retail, logistics and taxi-driving could be eliminated by advancing technology, there remains an insistence that jobs in 'high value' services will somehow remain immune. Here too, however, the evidence increasingly indicates the truth is rather different.

Speaking at a technology event in 2017, Mark Cuban, the billionaire owner of the Dallas Mavericks, predicted that the world's first trillionaire will be whoever masters commercial applications for AI, the reason being that artificial intelligence could prove particularly lucrative when applied to traditionally 'white collar' industries like insurance, software development or accountancy. 'I would rather be a philosophy major,' Cuban said of those training to enter such professions today.

Attention-seeking? Perhaps. Hyperbolic? Absolutely. Wrong? Probably not, because from cardiac surgery to calculating taxes, historically well-paid professions are just as repetitive and subject to the division of labour, and therefore automation, as anything else.

Take the da Vinci surgery robot. In 2017, University College London announced that this relatively low-cost machine had saved the lives of around 500 men with prostate cancer. While the robot itself is not automated – it instead grants a human surgeon far higher levels of dexterity and precision – the paths to automating a range of its regular operations resemble the blueprint for a self-driving car: you give a powerful data processor huge amounts of information, machine learning and a scalpel. The first part allows algorithms to model and reproduce outcomes and work their way through highly repetitive tasks, while the second allows for immediate and smart responses to unexpected situations.

In medicine, you can see how that would be applied to pretty much anything – from eye examinations to treating prostate cancer or taking blood. In areas more dependent on pattern recognition, such as radiology, machines have even more of an advantage. Radiologists use medical images like X-rays, CT and PET scans, MRIs and ultrasounds to diagnose and treat patients. While the field has greatly improved patient care over the last few decades, it has contributed to escalating costs and is relatively labour intensive. That is, until now.

Arterys, a medical imaging system, reads MRIs of the heart and measures blood flow through its ventricles. The process usually takes a trained professional forty-five minutes, but Arterys can do the same task in around fifteen seconds. Incredibly, it has a self-teaching neural network which constantly adds to its knowledge of how the heart works with each new case it examines. It is in areas such as this where automation will make initial incursions into medicine, boosting productivity by accompanying, rather than replacing, existing workers. Yet such systems will improve with each passing year and some, like 'godfather of deep learning' Geoffrey Hinton, believe that medical schools will soon stop training radiologists altogether.

Perhaps that is presumptuous – after all, we'd want a level of quality control and maybe even the final diagnosis to involve a human – but even then, this massively upgraded, faster process might need one trained professional where at present there are dozens, resulting in a quicker, superior service that costs less in both time and money. In an ageing society such advantages won't just be welcome, they'll be necessary.

A similar phenomenon is unfolding with law and legal services – a historically middle-class part of the service economy. According to a 2016 study by the consultancy Deloitte, 114,000 legal jobs in Britain – around 40 per cent of the entire sector – are likely to be automated over the next twenty years. That same study found technology had already eliminated 31,000 jobs in the industry. These tended to be lower-level positions, as intelligent search systems are increasingly preferred to junior lawyers and paralegals in a number of areas, especially those most engaged in repetitive searches or processing extraordinarily large amounts of information.

If Deloitte is correct, then the more repetitive elements of the legal industry are about to be widely automated. As with medicine it is beyond doubt that some jobs will remain, at least for a generation, but what both examples reveal is that historically white-collar jobs are just as exposed to trends which have already wrought a more obvious impact elsewhere in manufacturing.

Even an optimistic view sees sectors leading to net job creation as few and far between. Geriatric care – which combines high levels of fine motor coordination with affective labour and ongoing risk management – is one; after all, societies around the world will be affected by ageing populations over the course of the twenty-first century. Health and education generally will remain labour-intensive and, at the very least, will take longer to disappear. Even with these growth areas in mind, however, the overall picture of job losses due to automation makes standing still seem wildly optimistic.

The Future of Work

Not everyone agrees that progress will lead to peak human in the Third Disruption as the steam engine and fossil fuels led to peak horse in the Second. Indeed, two of the leading voices in the field of work and technological change, Erik Brynjolfsson and Andrew McAfee, believe value will instead increasingly derive from the generation of new ideas. So while anything repetitive may well be automated or significantly augmented by machines, the uniquely human skills of creativity and emotional connection will underpin the jobs of tomorrow.

This may well prove the case in some areas but surely not for a world of nearly 10 billion people. No doubt some new professions will expand — like solar cell engineer and wind turbine technician — while uniquely creative vocations, like chef or interior designer, will abide longer than others. But these can't compare to driver, cashier or construction worker in terms of the historic volume of work they create. Given the evidence from the last century, such a prospect would appear remote.

What seems more likely is that just as peak horse took more than a century to unfold after the arrival of Watt's steam engine a similar transition, uneven and intermittent, is presently underway. Now, just as in London in 1894, we must grasp the opportunities of the new world, rather than dwell on those technologies and social mores which are falling into the slipstream of history.

5

Limitless Power: Post-Scarcity in Energy

It never ceases to amaze me how PV costs keep coming down ... it is unparalleled in the history of energy use to have a source keep getting cheaper and cheaper and cheaper year on year not by single-digit, but by double-digit gains.

Danny Kennedy, managing director
of the California Clean Energy Fund

Energy and Disruption

Energy and its various sources profoundly shaped the First and Second Disruptions. As hunter-gatherers our means of survival were our own bodies, and we used them to create tools and source food. We inhabited a world without much technology, with the large brains of our ancestors mainly employed for complex spoken communication. Forms of concentrated energy, characteristic of societies capable of generating mass surplus, remained minimal.

That changed 12,000 years ago with the arrival of agriculture. Now humans began to domesticate other animals, breeding them not just for meat, skins and fur, but also their ability to perform tasks. This led to a major surge in productivity, making sedentary and increasingly sophisticated societies possible. One consequence of that complexity was the emergence of human slavery, a significant basis for social hierarchy and economic production during antiquity. These biological sources of energy – human and non-human – were later joined by technologies constructed around the elements, with the water and windmill increasingly common sights across Europe a thousand years ago.

Yet all of these innovations, both social and technological, were limited by their dependence on nature: the location and number of mills was determined by the availability of water and wind, while animals and humans were often unreliable and themselves difficult to maintain. While, by the early Renaissance, major advances were observable in fields such as printing, astronomy and navigation, methods of transport – as well as means of artificial light and heat – remained much the same as a thousand years earlier. While sixteenth-century Florence – the cradle of the European Renaissance – is upheld in the popular imagination as the embodiment of cultural refinement, when Niccolò Machiavelli wrote his *Discorsi* on the histories of Livy the world he inhabited differed surprisingly little to that of his first-century hero.

Towards the end of the eighteenth century this changed dramatically. The arrival of Watt's steam engine quickly provided an abundant supply of efficient, reliable power, in turn giving rise to novel industrial practices and patterns of consumption. While much is made of this being a technological and economic transformation – and it was – it also represented a rupture in energy. From now on, industrialising economies would depend on fossil fuels.

While most of the consequences unleashed by all of this

in culture, science and politics were apparent to anyone who lived through it, perhaps the most important after-effect would remain hidden for another two centuries. Industrial capitalism, whose immense powers were made possible by the extraction and burning of fossil fuels, would change the Earth's ecosystems. For the first time in billions of years, the activity of a single species would become the leading factor in our planet's ability to sustain life.

Arrival of the Anthropocene

While the precise environmental consequences of the Second Disruption are unclear, the scientific consensus indicates that higher concentrations of greenhouse gases, particularly carbon dioxide, have caused global temperatures to rise. As a result the world is 0.8 degrees centigrade warmer today than it was in the 1880s.

Because there is a delay between atmospheric composition and climate change, future warming is inevitable simply by virtue of past action. Furthermore, emissions of these gases have never been higher, meaning our world will proceed to get much warmer still – the key question being how much and how quickly.

And therein lies the problem with the politics of climate change. While we can be certain it is happening, almost everything else is speculation. Informed opinion agrees that global temperatures will rise by at least a further two degrees as a delayed response to present conditions. What remains unknown, however, is the time frame within which that will unfold as well as the precise consequences of such change – be it extreme weather events, rising sea levels or desertification.

Which means it is almost equally plausible that the world will warm by two degrees over the next several decades or centuries. In the context of the Earth being more than 4 billion years old such a difference is so small as to be the margin of error. For the human mind, however, and by extension the politics of global warming, it is everything. Any prediction that is deemed 'inaccurate' is a weapon for vested interests to discredit the notion of global warming altogether.

This is absurd when considering climate change not only as a political challenge, but an existential threat to our species. Even if warming remained below two degrees — something viewed as increasingly unlikely — it would represent an almost indescribable disaster. Anything beyond that, though, could be cataclysmic, creating a cascade of feedbacks concluding in a world unable to maintain multiple species — including us.

Can We Survive Climate Catastrophe?

What might such a sequence of events look like? A reasonable template might be the last time our planet was three degrees warmer than today, as it was some 10 million years ago. Then, sea levels were twenty-five metres higher than at present, with continental glaciers entirely absent from the Northern Hemisphere.

In this world, much of the Amazon basin would become a desert, and the glaciers which provide drinking water for much of China and the Indian subcontinent would all but disappear. The southern belt of the United States, countries bordering the Mediterranean — not to mention the Middle East, Australia and much of Africa — would become too hot to sustain their present populations. Alongside all of this, there would be a major rise in extreme weather events and a profound disturbance to the hydrological cycle. Here 'once in a century' weather events would be happening all of the time, with the previously extreme becoming routine. In this respect the 2017 Atlantic hurricane season with Hurricanes Irma and Harvey in particular, not to mention the sweltering summer of the following year, provide a glimpse of the future.

Even this isn't the worst-case scenario, however. An Earth six degrees warmer than today would have sea levels as much as 200 metres higher than they presently are with the oceans themselves too warm to sustain much life. This world would be almost entirely covered by desert, with only today's polar regions capable of supporting extensive agriculture. Yet even all of these challenges would be trivial compared to the real game-changer: substantially increased levels of atmospheric methane. In that event, anything with lungs would struggle to breathe.

The good news is we can still avoid much of this. Indeed, we may even be able to reverse some of the damage we've already caused, thereby undoing changes which at present appear inevitable. It won't be easy, however, and will require a global transition away from fossil fuels over the next two decades. Yet if humanity can reduce carbon dioxide emissions by at least 85 per cent by 2050 that should stabilise atmospheric levels at around 400 parts per million (ppm) – slightly above those of today but enough to steer clear of runaway catastrophe.

The bad news is that while we know what needs to be done, that's been the case for the last twenty-five years – and we've only gone backwards. The Rio Earth Summit, held in 1992, was the moment climate change became a story of global significance. Yet CO_2 levels were 61 per cent higher in 2013 than they were in 1990, with the years following the 2008 crisis recording the highest annual increases in history. Properly understood, our present course isn't one of inaction, it's rushing full speed to oblivion.

Energy Wants to Be Free

Right now, the world's human population consumes seventeen to eighteen terawatts of energy every hour, approximately 150,000 terawatt Hours (TwH) per year. While not evenly distributed by any measure, that means the average person is using about two kilowatts of constant energy, more or less the same as having a kettle switched on all of the time.

Over the next three decades those figures will substantially increase. The UN expects the world's population to rise to 9.7 billion by 2050, 2 billion more than today, with almost all of that increase coming from the poorer countries of the Global South. What is more these populations will increasingly consume energy, for heating, transport, home appliances and holidays, on par with the Global North. Switching the present global economy to renewables seems an immense task on its own, but the reality is even harder: we'll have to decarbonise a planet that uses twice as much energy as we do right now.

It is not all bad news, however. While increased energy consumption has correlated with economic growth for the last two centuries, demand for energy in the world's richest countries has started to decline over recent years. In the UK for instance, energy consumption peaked at the turn of the millennium, and has fallen by 2 per cent every year since. This means that despite higher living standards and a larger population, Britain's energy use in 2018 is actually lower than it was in 1970 – this in a country far from energy poor. Right now each person in Britain is consuming around three kilowatts of energy constantly, 50 per cent more than the global average.

While the UK's decline on this measure is more dramatic than anywhere else, it reflects the rule rather than the exception. European countries recorded an 8 per cent reduction in energy consumption between 2005 and 2013, while the US saw a fall of 6 per cent in the eight years to 2012. While the global relocation of manufacturing during the last forty years explains these changes to some extent, it is clear they are primarily a consequence of increased energy efficiency. It seems that just as with population growth, developed economies experience a ceiling in regard to energy consumption.

In light of these two facts – substantially increased consumption and a ceiling once a certain level of development is reached – it seems reasonable to use the per capita demand of the UK today as a template for the rest of the world in two decades. If anything, this is overly conservative – after all Britain is a comparatively wealthy country with a high standard of living and relatively cold climate.

A world two decades from now with 9 billion people, where each person uses the same energy as the average Brit does at present, would mean constant global consumption of around thirty terawatts of energy – 290,000 TwH a year, slightly less than double what it is right now.

While this forecast is higher than predictions elsewhere (British Petroleum foresee global demand of twenty-three terawatts by 2035), being generous with projections makes sense. Any transition to renewables should not be viewed as needing less energy than at present. After all, if we are serious about making a transition sufficiently quickly to prevent catastrophic warming, a large margin of error matters.

Of paramount importance is that decarbonisation start immediately. In 2017 the International Energy Agency announced the beginning of 'decade zero', saying that if a global transition away from fossil fuels didn't start over the next ten years, warming beyond two degrees would become close to certain. The following year the IPCC repeated those sentiments, concluding wide-scale decarbonisation had to begin before 2030 to avoid 'catastrophic' climate change in excess of 1.5 degrees centigrade.

This means that beginning in 2020, the wealthier countries of the Global North must initiate a transition to renewables, cutting CO_2 emissions by 8 per cent each year for a decade, aiming to completely decarbonise by 2030. At that point the countries of the Global South will embark on the same journey at the same pace. This will mean that by 2040, in spite of growing populations with rising expectations, they will have transitioned too. So in a little more than two decades, the world can go beyond fossil fuels in meeting all of its energy needs – not just electricity.

While that will be insufficient to stop warming of at least one degree, all the data indicates it will mean avoiding further calamity. What is more, it sets humanity on the path to virtually limitless energy that is permanently cheaper. Because unlike wood, coal or oil, the sun produces more energy than we can possibly imagine.

Solar Energy: Limitless, Clean, Free

The amount of solar energy constantly hitting the Earth's atmosphere is around 174 petawatts (1.740×10^{17} watts). Of this, approximately half hits the planet's surface. Humans currently consume less than 20 constant terawatts a year, meaning that many thousands of times more energy furnishes our planet than we currently require. Indeed the energy of the sun is so immense that despite being millions of miles away, in just ninety minutes the Earth is hit with the equivalent energy all of humanity uses in an entire year.

This means something profound: nature provides us with

virtually free, limitless energy. Like a nuclear reactor fixed at the centre of our solar system, the Sun is responsible for every organism you'll ever see. Virtually all life on Earth, from bacteria to trees, plants and, yes, you, results from a series of chemical reactions whose genesis was powered by solar energy.

While humanity has possessed the technology to capture and store this energy for decades, until recently it remained uneconomical and inconvenient compared to fossil fuels. Yet in the opening decades of the twenty-first century that has begun to change, meaning that just as the Third Disruption is powered by extreme supply in information and labour, the same also applies for energy.

A Quiet Revolution

Perhaps it should come as no surprise that solar energy has been with us since the earliest days of the Third Disruption, with photovoltaic cells first used on NASA's Vanguard 1 satellite in 1958. While an impressive feat of engineering, each panel only generated a maximum half watt at a time, meaning energy cost per unit was many thousands of dollars – far more than fossil fuels. By the middle of the 1970s, and as a result of the experience curve, that figure had fallen dramatically to around $100 a watt – still uncompetitive, but an eye-catching improvement.

More recently, however, solar costs have changed beyond all recognition with compounding improvements in price-performance meaning a watt of solar energy in sunnier countries can cost as little as fifty cents. Few disagree that this trend is only set to continue, and with global solar capacity doubling every two years – it increased by a factor of one hundred between 2004 and 2015 – it is likely that the dividends of the experience curve have much further to go. Installations of PV have grown by 40 per cent every year over the last few decades while in the UK, remarkably, 99 per cent of solar capacity has been installed since 2010.

It's little wonder, then, that by 2016 solar power was the fastest-growing source of new energy installations worldwide, outstripping the growth of all other forms of power for the first time. While renewable energy accounted for two-thirds of new power added to the world's grids that year, the International Energy Agency (IEA) found solar was the technology that shone brightest.

The prospects for solar haven't always seemed so positive. As recently as 2014, the IEA concluded that in the event of current trends persisting through to 2050, 'the best case will lead to generating costs lower than five US cents a kilowatt.' Within months of publication, however, that forecast was revealed to be unduly pessimistic. By 2017, the cheapest unsubsidised US solar contract was already below six cents a kilowatt and it now seems inevitable that by 2020 – thirty years ahead of schedule – the cheapest solar in the United States will be below three cents a kilowatt rather than five. If correct, that would mean it makes financial sense for virtually every home on Earth to install PV cells – even in cloudier Northern Europe.

Indeed, just a year after that report Deutsche Bank claimed solar had reached 'grid parity' in half of the sixty countries it analysed, predicting further price falls of 30 to 40 per cent before the end of the decade. In plain English that means that by 2020 new installations of solar cells – almost anywhere in the world – will generate cheaper power than a newly built plant that burns fossil fuels. In 2018 the International Renewable Energy Agency (IRENA) repeated that prediction claiming all renewables will be competitive with fossil fuels by 2020. They concluded how turning to renewable energy 'is not simply an environmentally conscious decision, it is now – overwhelmingly – a smart economic one'.

So while solar presently provides little more than 2 per cent of the world's electricity, trends observable for more than a decade indicate this is set to change dramatically – especially in those parts of the world where parity with fossil fuels will be achieved over the next ten years. Were the 40 per cent annual growth rate which has persisted over the last half century to continue through to 2035, that would mean global solar capacity of 150 terawatts – meeting not just the world's electricity needs but, on those projections outlined already, humanity's entire energy requirements. Were that trend to slow down in the coming years, as is common with the progression of any experience curve, it remains reasonable to predict a complete global transition to renewables sometime in the 2040s. Glimmers of that are already in evidence: in 2010, 2 per cent of UK electricity came from renewable energy, by late 2018 that figure was 25 per cent. Even more impressive is Scotland, a nation presently on track to completely source its electricity from renewable energy by 2020.

While that projection is staggering enough, even more incredible is that transitioning to solar will require no net increase in spending. Moving to clean, abundant energy is cost neutral. And that's before it gets permanently cheaper.

Here's how that is possible. The world currently spends around $2.2 trillion on fossil fuels every year. If today's demand of 15–17 terawatts doubled over the intervening period, that would mean compounded energy costs of around $80 trillion by the early 2040s. The UN has put a price on a complete transition to renewables, with their figure coming in at $1.9 trillion every year for forty years – which works out at slightly less than what would otherwise be spent burning oil, coal and gas to keep the world moving.

Yet those numbers might even be too kind to fossil fuels. They presume that oil and gas will stay at their presently low price for several decades into the future, something without historical precedent. Even if you take away climate change, solar and wind makes more business sense than the status quo.

And just as with automation and work, the ground zero for where the Second and Third Disruptions will converge will once more be in transport, with the autonomous electric vehicle solving as many problems as the automobile did when it replaced the horse. A few short decades from now, the seemingly terminal problems of today will appear as absurd as the London manure crisis of 1894 does to us.

Racing to the Future

In the summer of 2017 the British government announced it would ban the sale of all petrol and diesel vehicles by 2040. While well-intentioned, that lofty ambition failed to account for a crucial point – with current trends there will be none left to buy.

The reason why is that the cost of energy storage technologies, specifically lithium-ion batteries, are falling at an even-faster rate than solar cells. In 2009 Deutsche Bank reported the cost of lithium-ion batteries as $650 per kilowatt hour, predicting that figure would halve by 2020. Just like the IEA's solar energy forecasts in 2014, however, those predictions were way off, with the price of the technology falling 70 per cent over the following eighteen months. As a result, Tesla now expects to produce batteries for $100 per kilowatt hour by the early 2020s, although privately shareholders are told it could happen in 2019, while GM expects the same by

2022. In the last fifteen years the energy capacity of lithium-ion batteries has tripled, and the cost per unit of stored energy has fallen by a factor of ten.

The consequences of such shifts are hard to overstate. If Tesla and GM's forecasts are correct, then by the early 2020s a battery pack for a new electric car with a range of 200 miles could cost as little as £5,000. That would make the price of electric cars directly competitive with petrol versions while remaining on a downward curve. That is before considering how they'll be cheaper to run, insure and maintain over the course of their life. A generation from now, purchasing the energy powering your car may seem counter-intuitive, and a generation thereafter it will border on absurd.

That energy storage technology is subject to the experience curve just as much as renewable generation is important, because in any transition beyond fossil fuels – and towards extreme supply, where it becomes permanently cheaper – both will be necessary. If the experience curve persists across both, even just for another decade or two, the paradigm shift in energy will be every bit as disruptive as the rise and diffusion of fossil fuels after the early 1800s.

Solar and the Global South

Given renewable energy is a twenty-first-century technology, many would presume its effects, as with the mobile phone and internet, will be felt most profoundly across the Global North – at least initially. And yet it is in the poorer countries of the Global South where renewables, especially solar, will prove most transformational. In the right political framework they could even end the historic imbalance, present since colonialism and profoundly deepened by the Second Disruption, between the world's wealthiest and poorest nations.

Take Nigeria. The most populous country in Africa, half of its 180 million citizens presently lack access to electricity. As is common across the continent, the country is not only poor but experiencing a demographic boom, and some forecasts estimate that by the middle of this century it could have a population of more than 400 million people. What is more, tomorrow's Nigerians will rightly expect a higher standard of living than their forebears of today. But with fossil fuels that wouldn't just prove catastrophic, it likely isn't possible.

Which means the only way Nigeria, by 2050 possessing a larger population than the United States, will be able to provide universal access to electricity is solar power. Such a transition offers the opportunity to leapfrog some of the world's wealthier countries, enjoying cheaper energy with barely any of the sunk costs associated with extensive national grids. The same holds true for other developing countries which will similarly see rapid population growth alongside rising energy demand.

Instructive of how renewable energy may diffuse across presently low-income, energy-poor countries is the precedent set by the mobile phone. At the turn of the millennium there were a quarter of a million active mobile phone contracts in Nigeria, far fewer than the 600,000 landline connections. If you said then that access to a phone would be commonplace within two decades – in the absence of costly new infrastructure and with even the spread of electricity remaining mixed – you would have been laughed at.

And yet today Nigeria has 150 million mobile phone subscriptions – far exceeding the 200,000 fixed phone lines in active use. Meanwhile half the country has access to the internet. Importantly, this high level of connectivity has developed in a different manner to wealthier countries across Europe and North America. Rather than copying the sequence of infrastructure seen there – adopting the landline and then the mobile phone – Nigeria simply leapfrogged the former technology and adopted mobile internet en masse.

No technology has ever scaled as quickly as the mobile phone. It has allowed millions of people to open bank accounts in Kenya and Tanzania, register to vote in Libya, and access agricultural information in Turkey. Research reveals that mobile phone use is as common in Nigeria and South Africa as it is in the United States, with about 90 per cent of adults owning one – making it the most rapidly adopted technology in history. As recently as 2002, around 64 per cent of Americans possessed a mobile phone, a figure now beaten in places such as Tanzania, Uganda and Senegal. While these remain low-GDP countries, such a rapid spread of a technology which, only fifteen years earlier was viewed as the exclusive preserve of the global rich, is a significant development.

If the world is to completely decarbonise over the next twenty-five years, something similar will have to happen with solar generation and storage technologies. Just as with mobile since 2000, the adoption of renewable energy in poorer countries will be modular and distributed. Modular because solar cells and lithium-ion storage can be easily added to or upgraded, and distributed because generation and storage will often happen at the level of the household or street rather than a distant power station or energy hub. All of this is possible because of the good fortune of geography: despite being among the poorest countries on Earth, those nations near the equator – in Africa, Central America and Asia – enjoy sunshine like nowhere else. Now, with the onward drive of the experience curve across a range of renewable technologies, we are coming close to a tipping point – where nature's gifts become an economic blessing.

The numbers speak for themselves. In 2009 a radio, mobile-phone charger, and solar system sufficient to provide four hours of light and television a day would have cost a Kenyan $1000. Today it's $350 and falling. Each passing year not only brings energy closer to the world's poor, but energy far cleaner than fossil fuels and which is price deflationary – forever.

It's no surprise, then, that a new generation of businesses are looking to cash in on the convergence between rising electricity demand and declining costs for solar. One is M-Kopa, an American startup launched in Kenya in 2011. Today the company has half a million pay-as-you-go customers generating their own solar energy. The company's model is straightforward and, perhaps rather predictably, resembles the kind of contract associated with mobile phones. Customers pay a deposit of KES 3,500 (approximately $35) to take the system home and then a further KES 50 ($0.50) a day for a year before owning the system outright. Daily payments are made through M-Pesa, a mobile phone–based money system. Consumer renewable energy paid for by cashless, digital payments – the reality of African energy in the early twenty-first century.

Offering their products through a network of licensed dealers across Kenya, Tanzania and Uganda, the company's latest 'M-Kopa 4' package offers an eight-watt solar panel that charges appliances through USB ports, as well as two LED bulbs with light switches, a rechargeable LED torch and a radio.

One of M-Kopa's competitors is d.light, who boast offices in California, Kenya, China and India. They claim to have sold more than 12 million solar light and power products across sixty-two countries, the aim being to provide cheap, solar-powered electricity to 100 million people by 2020.

Another operator in the field is Off-Grid, whose model is similar to that of M-Kopa, the company providing the financing as well as the infrastructure to consumers. In Tanzania customers pay a deposit of around thirteen dollars to buy Off-Grid's cheapest starter kit: a panel, a battery, a few LED lights, a phone charger and a radio. They proceed to pay approximately eight dollars a month for three years, after which they own the products. Off-Grid's most popular bundle – for about twice the monthly price and a larger down payment – includes a few more lights and a flat-screen TV. As with M-Kopa, customers pay their bill by phone. All of this is made possible by the experience curve in solar cell and lithium-ion technology – as was the case with mobile phones over the last two decades – and it represents only the beginning for extreme supply in energy.

Just as solar technology has been getting cheaper, its performance has also been improving, and Off-Grid are planning for a point in the near future when their products are sufficiently powerful to have applications in industry such as pumping water for irrigation or milling cacao. This is partly thanks to the fact that solar is modular – you can simply add more capacity over time – as well as prolonged and impressive falls in its price–performance ratio. If the next decade sees change as rapid as the last, then it won't just be household appliances that are powered by solar energy in Kenya and Nigeria. Workshops, schools, restaurants and clinics will run on cheap, clean energy.

Such astonishing change isn't limited to Africa. Indeed the consultancy firm KPMG anticipates that a similar consumer model, allying increased credit with ever-cheaper technology, will mean that by as soon as 2025, 20 per cent of Indian homes will have some form of solar installation. And as bottlenecks like integrating larger solar farms with a patchy energy grid are overcome, India's renewable capacity is forecast to double by 2022 – overtaking even the European Union on growth.

If electricity sounds relatively unimportant, consider this: in the early twenty-first century hundreds of millions of women still face the risk of dying in childbirth because they have the misfortune of going into labour at night, surrounded by darkness and miles away from medical care. Even worse, 3 billion people still cook or access heat and light from biomass, primarily the burning of wood, dung and crop residue. According to the WHO this accounted for 36 per cent of global upper respiratory infections in 2002, 22 per cent of chronic obstructive pulmonary disease and almost 2 per cent of all cancers. In other words, transitioning to clean, renewable energy will, even just in the short term, save millions of lives a year – before it begins to play a decisive role in elevating the living standards of the world's poorest like never before.

Wind

Given as much as 80 per cent of the world's population inhabits areas with sufficient sunlight to rely exclusively on solar, it is obvious that in any transition beyond fossil fuels the focus will be on that particular form of energy.

But what about those colder countries with relatively large populations such as Russia, Canada and much of Northern Europe? Faced with the double-edged problem of far less sunlight and far higher energy requirements, particularly for heating, how can they make a similar shift to that which has already been outlined?

Part of the answer is energy conservation – and this holds true for all places regardless of solar exposure. While for now we might associate the idea of conservation with frugality and rationing, we shouldn't. In just a few years, saving energy – in your home, car and workplace – will be entirely automated.

The main reason why is the arrival of the internet of things.

Electric goods, including your car, won't just be communicating with one another, but distributing and storing energy in real time. If that sounds like an analogue to the internet, it is. Energy internets will soon be operating within and between households, and even everyday objects.

This will be centred around the car, the fulcrum of the transition to renewables in its earliest stages and the leading edge of the clean, autonomous economy. Cars won't just be data processors on wheels, they'll be giant portable batteries. And because the average electric vehicle uses around a sixth of its battery each day, there will be such an abundance of storage capacity that the majority of energy will still come from solar even in countries with little sunlight during the winter months. The same will apply to an increasing number of gadgets, not to mention homes, schools and workplaces. And where solar exposure makes that difficult, in places like Britain, increasingly efficient wind farms will make up the difference.

Indeed this is already starting to happen. In 2016 wind farms across the UK generated more electricity than coal power plants for the first time. That's all the more impressive when you consider the latter was responsible for more than two-thirds of the UK's electricity as recently as 1990. The following October, wind power in Scotland produced twice that nation's entire electricity needs.

Underpinning these shifts is the same thing powering the rise of solar energy – the experience curve. Just like progress with solar cells, development in wind turbine technology isn't showing any sign of abating. In 2017 the British government announced energy from offshore wind farms would be cheaper than that generated from new nuclear power stations as soon as the early 2020s. The implications of that announcement are hard to overstate. As recently as 2014, offshore wind in the UK was priced at £150 per megawatt hour, yet less than a decade later its price is set to more than halve, making it cheaper than Hinkley Point C – Britain's proposed new nuclear power station – before the foundations have even been laid.

And it doesn't end there. At some point during the 2020s, offshore British wind won't just be cheaper than nuclear power – it'll be cheaper than any alternative. One leading CEO predicted that Britain would soon generate half of its electricity from renewables, adding, 'When you look back ten years from now, we'll see this period around 2016–17 as an inflection point. The cost of offshore wind, also solar and onshore wind, is coming down at such speed that nobody could have predicted.'

Keeping Warm

Something else matters as much as energy – whether it's wind or solar – getting cheaper forever and vital storage technologies seeing dramatic falls in cost. That something relates again to energy insulation. Particularly for colder countries, the majority of household energy is expended on simply staying warm. In the UK, the average household heating system uses four times more energy than light and electricity combined. From a renewables perspective this is particularly concerning because energy demand peaks at the precise moment solar potential is at its weakest.

Yet even here the solution is relatively straightforward. Internal energy insulation – when done properly – means little to no energy need be expended on heating at all. Indeed, remarkably, we've known how to create buildings to such a standard for more than forty years.

In 1977, a group of Canadian researchers was contacted by the Saskatchewan provincial government to build a 'solar home' suitable to the local climate. Nearly airtight with triple-glazed windows, thick walls, roof insulation and one of the world's first heat-recovery ventilators, it remained cool in the summer and warm in the winter using virtually no energy. The Passivhaus was born.

Today Passivhaus is a voluntary standard for energy efficiency in construction, the objective being to reduce the environmental footprint of the building as much as possible. More recently developed in Germany and Scandinavia, passive design is not a supplementary detail to home building but a holistic approach seeking to integrate aesthetics, function and efficiency. It took off in the shadow of an insurgent green movement in 1980's Germany, with engineers and architects taking inspiration from the efforts of North American designers as they themselves responded to the oil crisis a decade earlier.

While we will always need energy for light, gadgets, transport and industry, the same isn't true for heating – certainly not on the scale we see today. Just because the transition to renewables will mean cleaner, more abundant energy than ever, that's no excuse to ignore potential improvements in energy efficiency. That's not to mention a big public health incentive. Across England and Wales every winter there are tens of thousands of 'excess deaths', primarily resulting from cold weather. Most of these could be avoided by implementing simple changes in homes and workplaces. Unlike renewable generation and storage what has stopped this from happening already isn't technology, but political priorities.

Another area which demonstrates how innovation isn't limited to energy generation and storage is light. At present, lighting accounts for one-fifth of UK electricity consumption. With LEDs, just as with improvements in solar cell, wind turbine and lithium-ion technology, we see the dividend of the experience curve in action once more, with the cost per lumen (the standard measure of visible light) falling 90 per cent between 2010 and 2016 alone. Indeed if all UK lighting was switched to LEDs, illumination would account for 3–4 per cent of overall electricity consumption compared to the 20 per cent it does at present.

The Solutions to Climate Change Are Here

There is no doubt about it – man-made climate change is a crisis whose magnitude is without precedent in human history. Equally true, however, is that we now stand on the brink of an energy revolution set to take us beyond the fuels which have so rapidly warmed our planet.

To mitigate the worst excesses of climate change, that revolution must now be accelerated. Not only is the enduring survival of our species at stake, but the very capacity of the Earth to sustain life. What is more, this opportunity extends beyond simply avoiding catastrophe, with extreme supply in energy potentially critical in severing the chains of under-development which, for so long, has held back the Global South. Riding the experience curve, technologies like solar cells, lithium-ion batteries, wind turbines and LEDs will mean permanently cheaper energy, ultimately not just outdoing fossil fuels but, as with information and labour, taking us beyond scarcity altogether. That is before we even develop the next generation of renewable technologies.

But as we've already seen, this is at odds with the essence of capitalist social relations, a system where 'the most basic condition for economic efficiency … [is] that price equal marginal cost' – that is, where things must be made for profit if they are to be made at all. That means one likely response to extreme supply in energy is that companies will try to make

the appropriate technology artificially scarce, market rationality requiring that at some point in the commodity chain
rationing (what is called excludability) has to be inserted.
If that sounds bizarre, it shouldn't. After all it was the very
issue that Larry Summers wrote about in 2001, and his recom-
mendations would ultimately inform how the entertainment
industries adapted to the challenges of extreme supply with
peer-to-peer distribution and file-sharing as they pursued
new business models like Spotify and Netflix. As the price
of energy, like labour and information, moves ever closer to
zero, there too it is likely we will pay through rents rather than
purchasing the good itself.

The evidence increasingly suggests that a transition to
renewables is coming. If that is accepted, the central question then becomes: how quickly, and with what ownership
models? Because it turns out that under the Third Disruption
it isn't just information and labour which want to be free – it's
energy, too.

6

Mining the Sky: Post-Scarcity in Resources

The Earth is a crumb in a supermarket filled with resources.

Peter Diamandis

A Finite World

The issue of resource scarcity and depletion is, alongside climate change, one of the central challenges of our age. While the sun may furnish us with more energy than we can possibly use, minerals like lithium and cobalt – needed to store solar energy in any post-carbon system – are ultimately limited. Which means that for any comparative advantages renewable energy does possess, it ultimately suffers the same problem as fossil fuels: ours is a finite world and we are fast approaching its limits. Regardless of the experience curve for solar cells, LEDs and lithium-ion batteries, without more minerals to build them, our future will still be one defined by scarcity.

Regardless of where our energy comes from, the problem of diminishing resources is now more pressing than ever. As a report by the Club of Rome, an organization that researches global limits, ominously noted in 2014: 'The production of many mineral commodities appears to be on the verge of decline … we may be going through a century-long cycle that will lead to the disappearance of mining as we know it.'

In this scenario coal production is forecast to peak by 2050, with 'peak copper' a reality a decade earlier. Lithium, a key mineral in what would be the mainstream technology for renewable energy storage, would quickly become strained in the event of wide-scale decarbonisation. While the Earth likely has sufficient quantities of it for a complete transition away from fossil fuels, even if global demand doubled, that would still require stockpiles to be continually recycled. While plausible – although at present only 1 per cent of batteries are processed in such a way – and no doubt an improvement, that is still a long way from post-scarcity and permanently cheaper energy.

That same report proceeded to outline how nickel and zinc, widely used in electricity storage, could face similar production peaks in just 'a few decades'. Though the lifespan of nickel mining might be extended for the best part of a century, it will be 'increasingly difficult and expensive to invest in and exploit.'

Perhaps the most alarming trend in mineral depletion, however, is phosphorus – an indispensable fertiliser in modern agriculture. While reserves of the chemical are far from low, only a fraction of it can ever be mined, meaning crop yields for 40 per cent of the world's arable land are already constrained by its limited availability.

Any shortage is particularly problematic in the broader context of declines in land productivity resulting from industrial agricultural methods which, in some places, have seen soil fertility fall by as much as 50 per cent. In 2014, researchers from the University of Sheffield claimed British soil had only 100 harvests left as a result of intense over-farming. At the precise moment the Earth's human population peaks in its demand for resources, the planet looks set to give up in exhaustion.

The present trajectory means not only will the world run out of fossil fuels, if we continue to use them, but even in the event of completely transitioning to renewable energy we will have to continually recycle multiple mineral resources. That might sound like a good thing, and it is, but it doesn't fit with what we know about the rapacity of capitalism and profit. In a world of more than 9 billion people, extracting resources as we do – killing people and destroying habitats in the process – simply won't be viable. Furthermore, mineral scarcity would just as likely give rise to resource conflicts as it would to cooperation and recycling. So even if information, labour and energy became permanently cheaper, the limits of the earth would confine post-capitalism to conditions of abiding scarcity. The realm of freedom would remain out of reach.

Except the limits of the earth won't matter anymore – because we'll mine the sky instead.

Asteroid Mining

In 2017 Elon Musk, CEO of SpaceX, unveiled the company's next step in conquering the final frontier. Speaking at the International Astronautical Congress, he announced the launch of the Interplanetary Transport System (ITS) – a new architecture consisting of a huge first-stage booster rocket, spaceship and refuelling tanker – all of which would replace the company's present systems. In a pivot away from commercial satellites and trips to the International Space Station, Musk outlined how the company's major ambition would be manned missions to other planets.

While space transportation might feel like the cutting edge of technology, no rocket has yet surpassed NASA's Saturn V – first launched in 1967. To this day it remains the tallest, heaviest, most powerful vehicle ever built. Its design and construction were overseen by Wernher von Braun, the engineer behind Nazi Germany's V2 rocket – the first man-made object to reach space. In the fifty years since, we have yet to see a more impressive machine than one whose construction was led by a man born before a plane even crossed the Atlantic.

In order to send humans to Mars, Musk's SpaceX will have to deliver precisely that. Enter the BFR – short for 'big fucking rocket' – the intended successor to SpaceX's Falcon 9 and Falcon Heavy boosters. Using a new family of Raptor rocket engines, the BFR will finally unseat Saturn V as the most impressive launch vehicle ever constructed. At the same time NASA is working on its Space Launch System which, when completed, will join the BFR in a new super-Saturn V category of spacecraft.

Birth of a Private Space Industry

Musk forecasts the first delivery of cargo to Mars using the ITS as soon as 2022, two years before the first humans set foot on the Red Planet. While his predictions are often right, Musk is notoriously late in delivery. That is partly a function of his business interests – renewables, electric cars and rockets – being at the cutting edge of industrial innovation. In reality, however, it is more an outgrowth of the South African's knack for raising interest through promising what seems undeliverable. While that is good for grabbing the media spotlight, it is bad for meeting deadlines.

But if you look at the story of SpaceX so far, you soon realise you'd be a fool to bet against him. Musk founded the company at the turn of the millennium, with NASA rudderless in the twilight years of the Space Shuttle programme and the romance of earlier decades drained from the industry. Then, the idea of commercial space transport was widely viewed as outlandish, and Musk a spendthrift eccentric.

Since then SpaceX has gone from strength to strength, achieving a litany of firsts. In 2008 it successfully launched the first privately funded liquid-propellant rocket into orbit – the stuff of science fiction only a decade earlier. In 2015, its Falcon 9 booster auto-piloted its return to Earth after launch, something without precedent for an orbit-capable rocket. That breakthrough was particularly important as many believe that reuseable first stage rockets will significantly lower the cost of sending a payload into space. A viable private market in off-world transport was ready to arrive.

Since then a glut of newcomers have emerged in the quest to push prices for space transport lower still. While they lack the means to conduct manned missions of their own, by providing cheap, weekly launch opportunities for low-Earth orbit, they will enter the slipstream of larger companies like SpaceX, Boeing and Jeff Bezos's Blue Origin.

One such company is Rocket Lab. Founded in New Zealand in 2009, it was the first private company in the Southern Hemisphere to send a booster rocket into space. Now based in the United States, its stated mission is to remove the barriers to mass space commerce by providing frequent, low-cost launch opportunities on its Electron booster rocket. While bigger players have their eyes fixed on manned missions to other planets, the fact that smaller outfits are capable of innovating in this area – albeit exclusively with smaller payloads – is remarkable. As the sector grows it will be companies like Rocket Lab that become the backbone of an incipient industry.

Falling Costs, Rising Ambitions

Winning the race to land on the Moon didn't come cheap. In today's prices the Saturn V's thirteen launches cost $47 billion over a decade – meaning each cost more than $3.5 billion. Launching twice yearly at its peak, the Apollo program came in at around $150 billion dollars accounting for inflation.

After Apollo, in order to reduce overheads and enable launches with greater frequency, NASA pursued the Space Shuttle program. Yet even that cost the US taxpayer half a billion dollars per launch, with the system enjoying no more than five flights a year at its peak. Since 2000 and the arrival of a private space industry, however, costs have fallen precipitously. Today a Falcon 9 rocket (much smaller than the Saturn V) costs SpaceX around $61 million to launch, while the larger Falcon Heavy is less than $100 million. Nevertheless, even those figures mean many companies and individuals stand little chance of reaching space, and even if they have the means to do so, there is currently a two-year waiting list for launch.

That could all change with Rocket Lab's commitment to launching every week on a projected cost of as little as $4.9 million per flight. That is only possible because of its uniquely efficient method of building and launching rockets: using the same amount of jet fuel a plane would need to go from LA to San Francisco, the Electron can put a payload into space.

The rocket's secret is its Rutherford engine, which takes many of the design innovations first applied by SpaceX further and deploying them on a smaller scale. Perhaps most remarkably, the Rutherford has an entirely electric propulsion cycle, using electric motors to drive its turbo pumps. In addition, it is the first oxygen-hydrocarbon engine to use 3-D printing for all primary components, allowing complex but lightweight structures unattainable through traditional techniques. As a result the company has not only reduced costs but decreased build time from months to days.

All of this also allows rapid scalability. As the company's CEO Peter Beck puts it, 'The vehicle was designed from the outset to be mass produced ... [we have a] 3-D-printed engine – with six printers [we] can produce one in twenty-four hours. So to scale up there we just buy more printers. The whole launch vehicle has been engineered and designed around manufacturability.'

Because its key technologies – from its high-performance electric motors and lithium-polymer batteries, to the 3-D printers used in construction – are on the same experience curve as the technologies outlined in the last chapter, these rockets will, like so much else, only get cheaper from here.

Rocket Lab isn't the only new player eager to use 3-D printing to reduce overheads in a still prohibitively expensive business. Relativity Space – like SpaceX, based in Hawthorne, California – wants to reduce the cost of a rocket launch from the $60 million mark to a fraction of that by simplifying production and all but removing human labour from building rockets, something which still accounts for as much as 90 per cent of overall cost.

The company's 3-D printers, with their eighteen-foot robotic arms, are among the largest ever built. Equipped with lasers that can melt a steady stream of aluminium wire into liquid metal ready for shaping, they represent a qualitative leap in the tools available to medium-sized businesses. The company's founders claim that by mid-2020 a handful of such arms will be able to build the entire body of a rocket, measuring ninety feet tall, seven feet wide and capable of carrying 2,000 pounds into orbit. They anticipate that construction time will take less than a month – and all for a booster which, while comparatively small, will be larger than SpaceX's original Falcon 1 rocket launched in 2008.

While the company aims to make its Terran 1 rocket operational by 2021, so far the printers have only produced a seven foot wide, fourteen foot tall fuel tank, which took several days, and an engine, which took a week and a half. Even if progress is slower than envisaged, which is likely, the design approach represents a paradigm shift. While NASA's space shuttle had 2.5 million moving parts, and SpaceX machines possess around 100,000, Relativity Space want their rockets to have a thousand moving parts or less – fewer than most cars. What is more, rather than having globalised supply chains they foresee the entire rocket being built in the United States.

Such an approach will almost certainly be industry standard in the near future. Blue Origin's New Shepard rocket has hundreds of parts which are 3-D printed, a figure that is constantly rising. This is leading to rapidly falling costs for potential newcomers, especially those looking to quickly prototype and iterate their designs. As Bob Richards from Moon Express said in August 2017, 'our first quotes from an unnamed aerospace company for our propulsion system in 2010 was $24 million in twenty-four months. We're now printing our engines for $2,000 in two weeks.'

All of which means that by the mid-2020s we can expect incredibly cheap, constantly improving rockets taking light payloads into space for a range of organisations. While the vast majority of their cargo will be ultra-small satellites, some will be exploratory landers capable of returning to Earth. Although progress will be intermittent, these trends will underpin the emergence of an industry set to define the twenty-first century: off-world mining.

Moon Express

In late 2017 Moon Express outlined their ambition to build a lunar base on the south pole of the Moon within three years. They will start by deploying a number of robotic explorers, ranging from their small MX1 to the larger MX9. All of these explorers will be powered by the 'eco-friendly' PECO engine, whose fuel will be drawn from basic elements found across the solar system – hydrogen and oxygen. This is critical because the greatest obstacle to a viable space industry is re-fuelling off planet. The PECO engine, and others like it, will need to operate in space with fuel produced wherever they find themselves.

The ambition is for these autonomous, unmanned vehicles to be deployed as either landers or orbiters. The MX9 is intended to deliver an MX1 to the Moon's surface, where it will make and then use fuel from lunar ice in order to return to Earth. That said, the name Moon Express shouldn't mislead you about the scope of the company's ambitions. While their initial target is the Earth's only natural satellite, the broader objective is to establish a self-sustaining architecture that can be used to prospect every planet, moon and asteroid in the solar system for resources. Naturally these primarily include minerals but, given the PECO engine will run on oxygen and hydrogen, ice as well. While mining metals like cobalt or platinum is the primary aim, the company also wants to transform the Moon, Mars – and anywhere else with substantial deposits of frozen water – into giant gas stations.

While the premise for most science fiction is that our descendants travel among the stars because of a desire to explore, to go where others have never been, the impulse driving all of this is far from altruistic. Nowhere is this clearer than in the 'Global Exploration Strategy' (GES) published in 2007, months before the first rumbles of the global financial crisis, by NASA and thirteen other space agencies. Detailed inside is the framework determining coordination among the most powerful countries in the world, establishing the basis for private enterprise to make profits in space in the not-too-distant future.

A decade later many of the document's presumptions are already apparent. It notes how space exploration 'offers significant entrepreneurial opportunities by creating a demand for new technologies and services ... space-based resource extraction and processing'. It even ventures into specifics, adding, 'Moon rocks are rich in oxygen that might be exploited to provide life support systems for lunar operations. Liquid oxygen can also be used as a rocket propellant – and it might be more economical to manufacture it in space than to lift it off the Earth.' In 2009 Nasa confirmed large quantities of water on the Moon, with the likes of Moon Express referring to the compound as 'the oil of our solar system'.

The framework proceeds to explicitly state how international cooperation in space will be undertaken to facilitate, rather than compete with, private interests: 'For business to be confident about investing, it needs the certainty of a long-term commitment to space exploration, the opportunity to introduce its ideas into government thinking, and the rule of law. This means common understanding on such difficult issues as property rights and technology transfer.'

In short, the GES showed how nation-states will agree on the rules for a new space race – one in which companies, rather than countries, will compete, and where the world's elite become even wealthier.

The Province of All Mankind

But where technology and market ideology is willing, the law may prove somewhat more difficult. The Outer Space Treaty, written in 1967 and ratified by over one hundred countries including the United States, remains the international standard for what humanity is permitted to do beyond the confines of Earth. That treaty specifically states that space is the 'province of all mankind', with countries unable to engage in 'national appropriation' or sovereignty over the Moon or other celestial bodies 'by occupation or by other means'.

That said, the treaty is a document of its time. Given it was forged in an era when only states had the capacity to engage in space exploration, and superpowers at that, it does not mention the rights and responsibilities of private business. Because there is no explicit prohibition preventing corporations from building or staking claims, mining in space could fall under legal parameters similar to those reserved for fishing in international waters.

Perhaps unsurprisingly then, Naveen Jain, co-founder of Moon Express, is optimistic on the legal issue, noting in 2011 how there 'is strong legal precedent and consensus of "finders keepers" for resources that are liberated through private investment, and the same will be true on the Moon'.

There is of course one problem with Mr Jain's thinking: 'private investment' is not responsible for our present level of technology, be it rockets, robotics, 3-D printing or other technologies critical to space exploration. Even now the most innovative private actor in the industry, SpaceX, remains dependent on NASA contracts to fund its research and development. What Jain wants, as we see repeatedly with the powerful, is to socialise the losses of publicly funded research and privatise the gains.

Even the wording 'liberated through private investment' grates, as if millionaires piggy-backing publicly funded research were acting for the greater good. Yet that is in keeping with market fundamentalism and, as Marx writes, the likes of Jain have viewed the bounty of nature as somehow the result of capitalism for centuries:

> Natural elements entering as agents into production, and which cost nothing … do not enter as components of capital, but as a free gift of Nature to capital, that is, as a free gift of Nature's productive power to labour, which, however, appears as the productiveness of capital, as all other productivity does under the capitalist mode of production.

To repurpose the phrase from capitalist realism: is it easier to imagine the end of the world than public ownership of the immense wealth beyond it? Why should it be?

For the first sixty years of space exploration, every significant breakthrough was achieved by nation-states. From von Braun's V2 rockets to the USSR's Sputnik and NASA's iconic Apollo missions, private investment had no influence in any of these technological developments. As a result, there is an overwhelming case for space to indeed be the province of all. The technologies which are set to bring its abundance within reach were funded by ordinary people – not wealthy investors.

Of course, that hasn't stopped certain countries trying to help domestic business interests at the expense of others. In 2015 Barack Obama legislated for American companies to engage in profitable off-world resource extraction for the first time – as long as those businesses are majority owned by US nationals. For now NASA formally maintains a neutral position on the matter, but the underlying reality is quickly changing.

That was clearly expressed in a sub-committee meeting for the US Senate Committee on Commerce, Science and Transportation convened in May 2017. Titled 'Reopening the American Frontier: Exploring How the Outer Space Treaty Will Impact American Commerce and Settlement in Space', its intended purpose was to test the limits of the Outer Space Treaty and maximise opportunities for private enterprise. Most indicative of this thinking was a speech given by Scott Pace, the executive director of the US National Space Council, towards the end of that year:

> It bears repeating: Outer space is not a 'global commons,' not the 'common heritage of mankind,' not 'res communis,' nor is it a public good … these concepts are not part of the Outer Space Treaty, and the United States has consistently taken the position that these ideas do not describe the legal status of outer space.

These are the words of people and institutions now gearing up for the major economic scramble of the coming century: who owns the resources and wealth of outer space.

The United States is far from acting uniquely in this respect. By January 2017 Luxembourg had already begun to create the legal frameworks for asteroid mining companies to base themselves in the Duchy, an offer quickly taken up by Planetary Resources – a company looking to establish itself as a key player in the industry.

This flurry of rhetoric, lobbying and legal activity should be expected. After all, we stand on the brink of a paradigm shift in resources. Some see that as a route to fantastic personal wealth. As Peter Diamandis, co-founder of Planetary Resources put it, 'I believe the first trillionaires will be made in space and the resources that we're talking about are multi-trillion-dollar assets.'

Beyond the Limits of the Earth

The existence of asteroids was confirmed at the dawn of the nineteenth century when, in 1801, the minor planet Ceres was observed for the first time. Scientists would soon come to distinguish asteroids from meteorites, the former having a diameter greater than one metre, the latter less than one metre. With comets, the difference is qualitative: while asteroids mainly consist of mineral and rock, they are composed of dust and ice.

Like the planets, asteroids orbit the sun, although few of them are purely spherical. The ones that are, such as Ceres, are often referred to as 'dwarf planets' as they are so large that their own gravitational mass has compressed them into a sphere. More generous estimates believe there may be 200 dwarf planets in the Kuiper belt of the outer solar system, as well as more than a million asteroids larger than a kilometre in diameter.

In terms of medium-term prospecting, however, there is a more interesting group of objects that reside far closer to home. At present we know of more than 16,000 near-Earth asteroids (NEAs) ranging in size from one metre to more than thirty-two kilometres. The number of NEAs more than a kilometre in diameter is estimated to be around 1,000, while the number of NEAs wider than 140 metres is around 8,000. Upper estimates speculate there are more than 1 million NEAs measuring forty metres in diameter or less, of which around 1 per cent have been discovered.

Whether it's Moon Express prospecting the Earth's only moon before moving on, or Planetary Resources sizing up NEAs, the potential abundance of off-world mineral wealth almost escapes comprehension. One estimate claims that a platinum-rich asteroid measuring 500 metres wide could contain nearly 175 times the annual global output of the metal, 1.5 times known world reserves. Even a smaller asteroid measuring the size of a football field could contain as much as $50 billion worth of platinum.

The asteroid belt likely contains some 825 quintillion tonnes of iron with 140 pounds of nickel for every tonne of iron. According to one estimate, the mineral wealth of NEAs – if equally divided among every person on Earth, would add up to more than $100 billion each. If we can access it, nature offers not only more energy than we can ever imagine, but more iron, gold, platinum and nickel too. Right now the resources we have access to are like a crumb in a supermarket. With the right technology mineral scarcity too would become a thing of the past.

The necessary advances to make asteroid mining a reality are steadily emerging. Japan's unmanned Hayabusa spacecraft successfully landed on the 25143 Itokawa asteroid in 2005, returning to Earth with samples of material from its surface five years later. In 2014 the Japanese Space Agency launched a successor mission, Hayabusa 2, with the asteroid 162173 Ryugu – widely viewed as the most cost-effective option for asteroid mining – its intended destination. Hayabusa 2 landed in June 2018 and is expected to return to Earth with samples some time in 2020.

Japan isn't the only country on the march when it comes to prospecting asteroids, however – in 2016 NASA launched OSIRIS-REx to study and sample the asteroid 101955 Bennu, with a scheduled return date of 2023. Unsurprisingly China has similar ambitions with the China National Space Administration looking to send and return a lander to the dwarf planet Ceres at some point during the 2030s.

But while most of the investment is coming from states, as has always been the case with space exploration, it is the private sector which is looking to reap the benefits. The leading actors in this embryonic field – Deep Space Industries and Planetary Resources – have chosen to adopt a similar approach to one another, focusing on prospecting asteroids through a mix of low-cost satellite technology and landers. DSI have developed what they call the Xplorer while Planetary Resources have a strikingly similar architecture which goes by the name of Arkyd. With local fuel generation and mining some way off, the aim with this opening round of products is to better understand the composition of target asteroids as well as identify deposits of ice which could, in future, be converted into propellant. As with Moon Express, the missing link is the ability to create fuel off-world in a process entirely free of human oversight. Given the rapid improvement of things like autonomous robots and vehicles since 2004 that is likely sooner than you think.

Indeed Chris Lewicki, CEO of Deep Space Industries, is optimistic on this issue, speculating that the first commercial extraction of water on an asteroid will happen by the mid-2020s. That, combined with the rise of regular, ultra-cheap launches, and increasingly sophisticated landers and robotics, will shape the opening rounds of asteroid mining. When combined with improvements in precision robotics – see the rapid development of the Atlas robot – an outline for the necessary technologies begins to emerge.

Once the likes of Deep Space Industries and Planetary Resources have prospected and claimed asteroids, and perfected methods to produce propellant from available ice, the industry will move from viable to profitable. This will be followed by a second round of products – extractors – which would use the propellant from asteroids to push them closer to

Earth for mining or – for those with particularly large concentrations of water – to create the 'gas stations' for a burgeoning industry looking ever farther outwards.

The Scramble for Space

A 2012 Caltech study concluded it could cost as little as $2.6 billion to move an asteroid into near Earth orbit for easier mining. That was confirmed in a 2017 report by Goldman Sachs which stated, 'while the psychological barrier to mining asteroids is high, the actual financial and technological barriers are far lower. Prospecting probes can likely be built for tens of millions of dollars each'. While $2 billion might sound like a lot, it is comparable to the sunk cost for a new rare earth mine, which MIT presently puts at around $1 billion. All of which means that once the full architecture is in place for asteroid mining, perhaps as soon as 2030, the marginal cost of each new mine will fall for every asteroid that is exploited. This will create a feedback loop of ever-improving infrastructure and rising incentives to extract minerals beyond our home planet.

That isn't to say asteroid mining doesn't have significant challenges to overcome before becoming a viable industry. Robots with the requisite levels of sensory-motor coordination are likely decades away although, as already highlighted in Chapter Four, that is more a question of when rather than if. Of greater concern is that the precise composition of asteroids, beyond predictive models based on broad categories, remains unknown. What if a company chose an asteroid only to find, upon arrival, that it holds far less water and platinum than expected? Between that and the immense costs required, specifically in robotics, it is difficult to see how nimble actors like DSI and Planetary Resources will fare when the likes of

SpaceX and Blue Origin will have more developed technology and far greater capital to risk.

Nevertheless, all of these problems can be surmounted – although as with all emerging industries how it will unfold is impossible to predict. But given the terrestrial challenges asteroid mining could address, primarily resource scarcity, as well as the new horizons it will undoubtedly open up, its rise over the coming century appears inevitable.

Abundance beyond Value

There is one final issue, however, that many in the industry appear unwilling to face. It is a problem born of success, much as the Horse Manure Crisis of 1894 placed the limits of the First Disruption against the abundance of the Second. It is also a problem born of extreme supply, which, as we've already seen, is difficult to reconcile with the price mechanism.

You see, there is so much mineral wealth beyond our planet, on other planets, moons and asteroids, that the moment off-world mining becomes a viable industry, the price of the very commodities investors had previously found so precious will collapse.

The most instructive example here is the asteroid 16 Psyche, located in the belt between Mars and Jupiter. Measuring over 200 kilometres in diameter, it is one of the largest asteroids in our solar system, composed of iron, nickel and rarer elements such as copper, gold and platinum. The 'value' of this giant floating mine? Around $10,000 quadrillion – and that's just the iron. To be clear, Psyche is a rarity. But it demonstrates a crucial point: mining space would create such outlandish supply as to collapse prices on Earth.

~

In August 2017 Peter Diamandis, co-founder of Planetary Resources, asked Blue Origin's Erika Wagner who would win in a fight between her boss, Jeff Bezos, and Elon Musk. 'So, Peter, let me tell you about what we're doing at Blue Origin,' Wagner diplomatically replied. 'We're really looking towards a future of millions of people living and working in space. The thing I think is really fantastic ... is that the universe is infinitely large, and so, we don't need any fisticuffs ... we're all going to go out there and create this future together.'

While Wagner is correct in identifying that our solar system has more mineral wealth than we can possibly imagine, the likes of Musk and Bezos aren't risking their personal fortunes – the former stood on the brink of bankruptcy multiple times while refusing to take SpaceX public – so that others can get rich. What is more, once the shareholder model is applied to companies like DSI and Planetary Resources, and their inevitable competitors, the emphasis will be on the rate of return rather than social progress.

As we've already seen with information in the early twenty-first century, under conditions of abundance capitalism pursues a form of rationing in order to ensure profits. Given the potentially limitless wealth made possible by asteroid mining, that same logic would be applied by private enterprise in the sector and their allies in politics.

As with information, and soon renewable energy too, that will necessitate the formation of temporary monopolies of some kind. How might this look? One answer is that private companies will prospect and claim the most valuable asteroids decades before even attempting to exploit them – something we are already beginning to see. Another might be intellectual property rights applied to certain technologies used for mining, perhaps in the process of converting ice to fuel, creating scarcity there instead. Finally, and perhaps most sensibly, one could foresee the adoption of predatory pricing for commodities mined off-world, with the price of each fixed marginally below the cost of operating the cheapest terrestrial mines. This would serve to keep drills turned off on Earth while maintaining price stability and guaranteeing huge profits for mining companies.

It isn't hard to imagine how this might be justified by big business and the political establishment, with off-world mining companies presenting themselves as custodians of the future. 'We have learned our lesson as a species,' they might say, internalising seemingly progressive arguments from the green movement. 'We have ruined one planet, we will never ruin others.' In the meantime, as Peter Diamandis has publicly predicted, those engaged in mining would join the ranks of the wealthiest people on Earth.

That isn't to say such abundant resources should not be managed responsibly, nor that we should exploit off-world mines as recklessly as we have treated the Earth. Rather, the Outer Space Treaty should be made clearer, in particular the rules concerning the exploitation of off-world minerals for profit. A template here might be the Madrid Protocol within the Antarctic Treaty System,* Article Three of which states the 'protection of the Antarctic environment as a wilderness with aesthetic and scientific value' shall be a fundamental considera-tion, while Article Seven adds, 'any activity relating to mineral resources, other than scientific research, shall be prohibited'.

Similarly, the Outer Space Treaty states that the explora-tion and use of outer space is 'the province of all mankind'. But lacking the clear language of the Madrid Protocol, the Treaty would appear to necessitate an international body to

---

* Addressing the General Assembly on 22 September 1960, President Eisenhower indeed proposed that the principles of the Antarctic Treaty be applied to outer space and celestial bodies.

ensure the fair distribution of wealth before private entities, like DSI and Planetary Resources, can take a thing. Indeed, President Eisenhower alluded to precisely that when, addressing the United Nations in September 1960, he proposed the world 'press forward with a program of international cooperation for constructive, peaceful uses of outer space under the United Nations'.

Space is indeed the province of us all, if for no other reason than the technologies which bring its abundance ever closer were impossible without public funding. The money spent on the International Space Station alone totals some $150 billion, a similar figure to that of NASA's Apollo missions.* From the V2 to Sputnik, and even today's SpaceX, the costs of space exploration have been socialised. It is only right, therefore, that the gains be as well. Private business was incapable of even launching a liquid-propellant rocket into orbit until 2008, sixty-four years after a V2 left the Earth's atmosphere. So much for private sector innovation.

Capitalism has a number of useful features. Yet none of its shortcomings match its inability to accept natural abundance. Facing such conditions for resources – as with information, energy and labour – production for profit begins to malfunction.

All of this can be explained by the fact capitalism emerged in a world fundamentally different to the one now coming into view. That meant it accepted a different set of presumptions – ones it took as permanent, but which were, in fact, contingent. Faced with a limitless, virtually free supply of anything, its internal logic starts to break down. That is because its central presumption is that scarcity will always exist.

Except now we know it won't.

---

* In 1973 dollars it was calculated to have cost $25.4 billion.

7

Editing Destiny: Age and Post-Scarcity in Health

We are as gods ... we might as well get good at it.

Stewart Brand

An Ageing Species

By 2020, for the first time in human history, there will be more people over the age of sixty-five than under the age of five. By 2050 there will be more people over sixty-five than under fourteen. This is perhaps the crowning achievement of our species — nowhere else in nature do the old outnumber the young.

While certainly welcome, such a shift brings with it numerous problems, not least that living longer, while having fewer children, imperils forms of collective insurance which presume a larger 'working age' population than dependents. Indeed, those first two conditions have, in many countries, already been met and are presently going global. What remains uncertain is whether public pensions and socialised elderly care will be viable in the future. If not, it would be ironic: capitalist affluence means more of us reach old age, yet many would lack the resources to be cared for.

In the middle of the seventeenth century the philosopher Thomas Hobbes described life in a state of nature, a hypothetical condition without government or rule of law, as 'nasty, brutish and short'. Those words, particularly the last, could have been applied far beyond the shores of Hobbes's England. Besides the issue of war in both his homeland and abroad – relative constants prior to the twentieth century but particularly severe in the 1640s – his was also a world absent of modern medicine and where adult men rarely lived beyond forty. By the mid-1800s, however, that had changed as the application of the scientific method to healthcare and hygiene saw the mortality rate of infants and children sharply decline. Previously high fertility rates, combined with more children surviving to adulthood, inevitably meant unprecedented population growth among those countries at the forefront of the Second Disruption.

The implications of this were profound. While it took hundreds of thousands of years for the world's human population to reach 1 billion by 1800, it would only be another hundred and twenty before it doubled once more. This proved to be just the start, however, and by the end of the twentieth century the Earth's human population had reached 6 billion, with forecasts for the middle of this century of around 9.6 billion. If confirmed that will mean the world's human population has increased tenfold in around 300 years.

Two other trends accompanied this surge in population. The first was extended life expectancy. By 2015 the average human, anywhere in the world, could expect to reach seventy-one years of age – an improvement of four decades on even the early twentieth century. The second was an inverse correlation, with fertility rates falling as a country becomes wealthier. Just as a country's population increases during industrialisation, this later self-adjusts as birth rates fall once a certain level of development is attained. Thus while the last two centuries have seen the world's population surge, and the time between respective doublings becoming successively shorter, this is now slowing down, and many expect the world's population to peak towards the end of this century. Just as with energy consumption, it appears that there is something of a 'natural' limit on demographic growth.

While this is positive from the perspective of distributing limited resources – in the mid-twentieth century many viewed the rate of population growth as liable to continue indefinitely – the challenges presented by societal ageing are, if anything, even greater.

That much was clear in a 2013 simulation conducted by the credit ratings agency Standard & Poor's which found that, as a result of ageing demographics, 60 per cent of the countries analysed were predicted to see their credit status reduced to junk within a generation. Their subsequent conclusion, unsurprisingly, was that the status quo was unsustainable and that major reforms, from increasing the pension age to shrinking the public sector, were necessary. A larger study published three years later revealed less pressing problems, concluding only a quarter of countries seemed destined for trouble as people lived longer and fertility rates continued to fall. Yet perhaps most notable about that second report's findings was the geographical spread of the countries it identified with the Ukraine, Brazil, China and Saudi Arabia all facing major problems ahead. It appears the prospective crisis of elderly care is bigger than any single economic model or set of cultural values.

What is more, ageing will diminish growth. In 2016 the

research division of the US Federal Reserve published a paper detailing how changed demographics will render central banks powerless to raise long-term interest rates. Citing an example based on the changing demographics of the United States it concluded, 'low investment, low interest rates and low output growth are here to stay ... the US economy has entered a new normal'. These trends are observable across the Americas, Europe and Asia. While the default policy response in recent decades has been calls for greater immigration (with a few exceptions such as Japan), given ageing is one of the inevitable consequences of the Second Disruption – an experience that has and will continue to visit every society – that is clearly inadequate. As Africa and Asia experience the same trends that Europe and America did before them, the call for economic migrants to make up labour shortages will increasingly be met with the response, 'from where?'

In most developed countries, particularly in Europe, lower growth is already rubbing up against higher spending. In the UK the costs of health and long-term social care, the state pension and other benefits are forecast to increase annual spending by 2.5 per cent of GDP every year in the decade after 2020. Between 2016 and 2030 Britain's population over sixty-five will grow by a third while its 'oldest old' – those over eighty-five – will almost double. While politicians perennially talk of 'balancing the books', in the context of demographic change – as well as a failed economic model – it is clear that under such conditions large budget deficits would be permanent.

Ageing in Britain: Austerity beyond Austerity

In 2017, Britain's Conservative Party lost their parliamentary majority. Seven weeks earlier when Theresa May called a snap general election, anything short of a landslide victory had seemed impossible. While there was much to commend in how Labour fought back from the brink, it is hard to ignore just how poorly the Tories fared – their nadir being one of the great unforced errors in modern politics: the 'Dementia Tax'.

While the proposal proved to be the election's turning point, it was as much a response to long-term necessity as political naivety. Its logic was simple: people who need social care should pay for it themselves until the value of their assets, including their home, reaches a floor of £100,000. While a family would never be forced to sell a property during a patient's lifetime – with the cost being recouped only after death – for many this was tantamount to introducing a new inheritance tax. That led to widespread anger, particularly among their voter base, because while seemingly progressive, the policy created a lottery in how medical services were paid for. If you had cancer the cost of treatment was socialised through the NHS, whereas if you had dementia you were on your own. The Tories included the policy in their manifesto, framing it as painful but necessary, because they incorrectly believed their lead to be unassailable.

And yet there was more to the Dementia Tax than political myopia. The emphatic changes it proposed, which so outraged long-time Tory voters and activists, at least represented a response to the crisis of ageing. Whoever governs, and whatever their ideological views, increased life expectancy and declining fertility rates – two trends which will ultimately impact every society – call into question the viability of socialised health and social care. June 2017 won't be the last time a major political upset is caused by the politics of ageing.

Any presumption that the leading causes of death will remain static over the next century ignores just how much has changed over the last hundred years. Where infectious diseases like tuberculosis and influenza were once the biggest killers of all, they have retreated, with age-related illness accounting for around two-thirds of global mortality every year.

Indeed by 2016 the leading cause of death in England and Wales was no longer heart disease, but Alzheimer's and dementia – a significant shift. Already the sixth leading cause of death in the United States, it is reasonable to expect that elderly dementia will become increasingly prevalent as life expectancy improves (already in 2013 it was forecast that the global rate of dementia would triple by 2050). Given the economic cost of the condition already – $818 billion in 2015 – it is clear that between squeezed public finances and a shrinking workforce relative to the elderly population, major change is inevitable.

Part of the reason why is that the challenges of ageing and healthcare are exponential.

Similar to how Moore's Law has meant extraordinary progress in digital technology, there is an exponential function between age-related medical conditions and the progression of years. This means ageing is a far greater issue than even pessimists might initially presume: the chances of suffering Alzheimer's roughly doubles between the ages of seventy and seventy-five, and doubles again between seventy-five and eighty. For progressively older societies, with ever-larger concentrations of the 'oldest old', this poses an unprecedented challenge. Even if we can mitigate or potentially cure things like cancer, heart disease and stroke, the sheer accumulation of conditions like Alzheimer's would ultimately prove too much to manage.

But here, as with the other crises of technological unemployment, climate change and resource scarcity, the Third

Disruption offers a solution which not only meets the challenge but goes well beyond it. As with those other responses – in energy, labour and resources – it is underpinned by the tendency to extreme supply.

The reason why is that while information 'wanting to be free' might initially seem limited to relatively marginal areas such as music, film and literature – as well as new forms of collective action and even automation – it is set to be of greatest importance of all in healthcare. Perhaps that shouldn't be a surprise. After all, every living organism is essentially a composite of material and information, the difference between the E. coli virus and your favourite pet a question of complexity and scale.

While digital information exists in the binary code of 0s and 1s, DNA is instead arranged in vast sequences of four types of nucleobase, abbreviated C, G, A and T. While over recent decades we have come to understand this biological data in ever-greater detail, we now stand on the brink of something even more remarkable: being able to easily change it.

(Genetic) Information Wants to Be Free

In 1953 Francis Crick and James Watson identified the molecular structure of DNA, 'the basic copying mechanism by which life comes from life' as Crick would later write to his son. The following year, the first functional silicon transistor was built. From there the development of these two fields would become increasingly connected, as improvements in our capacity to understand the basis of life and genetic instructions came to depend on the progress of digital technologies.

This culminated in 2003 when the Human Genome Project completed mapping all 3.2 billion base pairs of the human genome. Formally launched in 1990 with a budget of $3 billion, most of its progress was made in its final few years, enabled not only by improved techniques but massively improved computational power. Indeed, towards the end of the project it became increasingly clear that improvements in gene sequencing weren't linear but, like Moore's Law in computing, exponential. What is more, 2003 turned out to be just the beginning. Despite being an information technology from the start, progress in genetic engineering over preceding decades had trailed developments elsewhere in computing. Yet the momentum gained over those final years of mapping the first human genome decisively changed that, taking the prospect of gene therapies from the realms of plausible speculation to reality.

So while it took thirteen years and billions of dollars to sequence the first human genome, by 2007 the cost of performing the same process for a single individual had fallen to around $1 million, a far steeper fall in the price curve than any other information technology As with the rice on the chessboard, the further progress went the more incredible its improvements became. This meant that by January 2015 sequencing an individual's genome had fallen to $1000 and two years later the biotech company Illumina unveiled a machine it expected to do the job for under $100. Equally impressive as the improvements in price performance are how quickly the process takes: while it took thirteen years to map the first human genome, Illumina's machine performs the same task in under an hour.

If all of this sounds dizzying, that's because it should – since the turn of the millennium the falling cost of gene sequencing is even more astonishing than the exponential improvements of Moore's Law. While the performance of a computer chip per dollar is doubling every twenty-four months, the costs of sequencing a genome have fallen by a factor of between five and ten times a year. Even if that precipitous fall in price–performance slows down – perhaps aligning with trends elsewhere in computing for a further decade – sequencing a genome could cost as little as $30 by the late 2020s. That alone would transform healthcare, although according to Raymond McCauley, who previously worked at Illumina, such a conclusion is unduly pessimistic. His view is that by 2022 sequencing a genome will cost as little as flushing a toilet. In other words, it'll be too cheap to even think about.

Illustrative of just how quickly the field is changing is the Earth BioGenome Project. First proposed in February 2017, it is explicitly modelled on the earlier Human Genome Project. But while the achievements of its predecessor were historic, any equivalence downplays the sheer scale of the latter's ambition. Rather than map the genome of a human individual, the Earth BioGenome Project intends to sequence every life-form on Earth, from single-celled organisms to plants and complex mammals. While such an endeavour won't come cheap, at several billion dollars it will cost far less than mapping that first human at the turn of the millennium.

But what benefits would having your genome regularly sequenced actually bring? How would it help provide healthcare and meet the challenges posed by age-related conditions? Initially it would allow for the earliest possible detection of conditions such as cancer before outward symptoms were even discernible, moving the disposition of medicine from reactive to predictive. Here stroke, cancer and even the common cold would no longer come without warning but could be foreseen and dealt with in ways previously unimaginable. This predictive practice would, most likely, begin the moment you were born.

For millennia humans have had a panoply of birth rites

accompanying the arrival of a new child. Within the Islamic faith the call to prayer, or *adhan*, are the first words a baby should hear, while in Judaism a male infant should be circumcised eight days after birth in a *brit milah* ceremony. Across our planet new life is accompanied by ancient ritual. In the not-too-distant future, however, the first thing a newborn will be subject to – alongside various cultural customs – will be having their entire genome sequenced. Indeed, it is already common in a number of countries for a pinprick of blood to be taken at birth to test for conditions such as phenylketonuria (PKU) and cystic fibrosis.*

Expanding this to the entire genome, however, and then subjecting it to analysis by an AI would allow for the immediate isolation of risks specific to infant mortality, bringing this to fall even further. Relevant to the longer term it would create a detailed health profile – from allergies to risk of coronary heart disease and cancer in later life – as well as advising precision testing or treatments for conditions like asthma or short-sightedness. If that sounds like something for the distant future, it shouldn't – the US National Institute of Health is currently spending $25 million over five years trialling precisely such a treatment. And that's before the price drops to less than a bar of chocolate.

Remarkably this would be just the start for preventative medicine. It turns out that just as unborn children release their DNA in the bloodstream of expecting mothers, so do cancerous tumours. That means that tissue biopsies, used to investigate suspicious lumps, would be replaced with liquid ones where DNA in blood would be used to detect, track and treat cancer. As with biopsies the same process could replace

---

* In some cases, these diseases can be treated: any disability caused by PKU can be avoided by feeding the child a specific diet that prevents the build-up of phenylalanine (an amino acid) in the blood.

mammograms and colonoscopies, not just because of convenience and cost – but also effectiveness.

Besides significantly reducing cancer-related deaths, this
process would be relatively inexpensive and easily rolled out
across poor and wealthy countries alike. Meaning that just like
the mobile phone, low-GDP countries would quickly enjoy
healthcare services impossible in the most advanced nations
just a few decades earlier. At present our vision of first-class
healthcare is giant, expensive technology which can take up a
whole room – not unlike the computers of the 1960s and 1970s.
But from sequencing the genome of newborns to preventative
treatment for cancer, handheld genome sequencers will allow
for diagnostics that replace rooms' worth of equipment. As
with communications and energy infrastructures, the growth
of cutting-edge healthcare in the Global South will look very
different to existing infrastructure in places like Europe and
the United States. Once more the technologies of the Third
Disruption will effectively allow some of the world's poorest
countries to 'leapfrog' conventional parameters for development, meaning decades from now relatively poorer countries
could have rates of cancer detection more impressive than
the wealthiest societies of today. Whether they do, of course,
depends on the politics of how the technology is distributed.

If handheld gene sequencers sound outlandish – reminiscent, perhaps, of the 'tricorder' in *Star Trek* – then don't
worry, because they already exist. The $1,000 MinION
sequencer, which fits in the palm of your hand and weighs just
ninety grams, can sequence the genome of organisms such as
the Ebola virus multiple times and at high speed.* While the
technology can't yet deal with the complexity of an organism such as a human, given prodigious improvements in price

---

* It's worth pointing out that the genome of E. coli wasn't sequenced
until 1997, which represented the cutting edge of biotechnology at the time.

performance it is only a question of when such an innovation will appear.

But while gene sequencing will change the provision of healthcare – creating preventative medicine that permits us to respond to illness before we even exhibit symptoms – the biggest breakthrough in biotechnology will be gene therapies. In terms of the leading causes of death, whose primary risk factor is age, this will create abundance in healthcare which even exceeds the exponential challenges posed by societal ageing.

Extreme Supply in Healthcare: Gene Therapies

Genetic engineering is nothing new. Indeed, we have knowingly altered the genome of various species for 12,000 years through selective breeding – a central innovation of the First Disruption. That gave us creatures fit for labour and crops like wheat which were hardy, easy to grow and nutritious. While we gained mastery in these fields before we had cities, writing or mathematics it wasn't until the nineteenth century, through the work of Gregor Mendel, that we understood precisely how such mechanisms function.

After Mendel, however, understanding genetic inheritance increasingly resembled a science rather than an art. By the middle of the twentieth century our knowledge of the field was so impressive that humans grasped how they might be able to accelerate a process seen throughout nature – evolution – inside a laboratory. While DNA was understood to be responsible for heredity from 1952, and Crick and Watson's double helix model was formulated the following year, the first genetically-engineered animals weren't produced until the early 1970s. That breakthrough was arguably as profound as the transistor, the integrated circuit and even Watt's steam engine. Within just a few short decades theoretical science had become applied technology.

While of widespread popular interest and the basis for innumerable Hollywood films, this historic leap had little immediate impact in the provision of healthcare. The techniques required were prohibitively expensive and complex, meaning that for more than a generation advances in the field remained slow. But like anything subject to exponential development, what seemed like inertia soon gave way to a deluge of change.

Gene editing is a type of genetic engineering in which DNA is inserted, deleted or replaced in the genome of an organism. This is achieved by using restriction enzymes, or 'molecular scissors', of which – until recently – there had been three kinds: meganucleases, zinc finger nucleases (ZFNs) and transcription activator-like effector-based nucleases (TALEN). While there is significant variation in the price of each process, ZFNs and TALEN were developed more recently, all three remained out of reach for all but the wealthiest of institutions. Much like computers until the early 1970s, gene editing was the exclusive preserve of elite researchers and subject to massive overheads. As a result experimentation and trials were rare, expensive and slow.

That has changed in recent years, however, with the arrival of CRISPR-Cas9. CRISPR is a new approach which reduces the costs of gene editing by 99 per cent while cutting experiment times from months to weeks. While it is yet to be fully perfected and is not always sufficiently precise, CRISPR is a programmable and easy-to-use technique for almost any lab, allowing scientists to edit genetic information with unprecedented efficiency. Just like SpaceX and rocket technology, CRISPR-Cas9 doesn't permit humans to do anything particularly new. Rather, it illustrates how information wanting to be free disrupts mainstream views about scarcity and makes extreme supply possible. How we deal with biology, primarily our own, is set to be transformed just as radically as labour with automation, energy with renewables and resources with off-world mineral extraction.

The technique itself is both simple and elegant. That's because CRISPR, which stands for 'Clustered Regularly Interspaced Short Palindromic Repeat', imitates the immune mechanism of bacteria when attacked by a virus in nature. Confronted with such a situation, the bacteria will take strips of the virus's DNA and insert it into their own using an enzyme called Cas. These newly formed sequences are the CRISPR, which the bacteria then uses to produce RNA copies to recognise viral DNA and repel future attacks.

While these processes have been observed and understood since the early 1990s, it wasn't until 2013 that CRISPR was transformed into a tool suitable for gene-editing. That was achieved by replacing the bacterial CRISPR RNA system with a modified guide RNA which now acted as a signal to inform an enzyme, called Cas9, where to look. This allowed the enzyme to effectively scan a cell's genome to isolate a match before slicing it out. Applying this same process, scientists can change or add DNA within a cell in a manner reminiscent of cut, copy and paste – although, for now, a slight margin of error remains. Decades after confirming DNA is responsible for genetic inheritance, and more than sixty years since the invention of the silicon transistor, information technology can reprogram biological systems with increasing ease.

Already, governments in a number of countries including the US and UK have approved the use of CRISPR-Cas9 in human embryos and adults. You can even buy home kits online using the same system to modify bacteria in your spare time. Altering bacteria to glow in the dark like jellyfish or develop resistance to certain strains of antibiotics might have won a Nobel Prize thirty years ago – today children in middle school are doing it.

Trials with CRISPR-Cas9 have already yielded impressive results in laboratories across the world, creating 'buff beagles' without myostatin, preventing HIV infection in human cells, partially reversing the effects of Huntington's in nine-month-old mice, and slowing the spread of cancer. It seems increasingly likely that gene-editing in general – and CRISPR-Cas9 in particular – could help eliminate a number of genetically inherited conditions, and with over three thousand caused by a single incorrect letter in our DNA – including Huntington's disease, cystic fibrosis and sickle cell anaemia – that alone would represent spectacular progress. In the second half of the twentieth century humanity eradicated smallpox. In the first half of the twenty-first it could eliminate thousands of genetic disorders. Forever.

But the possibilities of gene editing go beyond mitigating, and even overcoming, genetically inherited conditions which impact hundreds of millions. The genome could be reprogrammed to become resistant or even immune to things like stomach flu, HIV and Alzheimer's as well as lowering the risk for coronary heart disease, having leaner muscle and possessing stronger bones. This might all sound a little much, and before editing the human genome at scale such efforts should be subject to vigorous public debate. But how much difference is there between improving nutrition for health outcomes and optimising our biological programming? Not much – and while pursuing both is likely ideal, the second is a lot more precise.

Since 2016 alone, the number of gene-editing trials deploying the CRISPR-Cas9 technique have substantially increased. With the overwhelming majority taking place in either China or the United States, and the latter now playing catch-up, some are now referring to this new rivalry as 'Sputnik 2.0'.

But while such a comparison is easy to understand, there is a seismic difference between innovations in biotechnology today and the Cold War clash for scientific supremacy a half century ago. For fifty years after Sputnik was launched in 1957, the cost of space exploration was so prohibitively high that only states, and superpowers at that, could afford to participate. Techniques like CRISPR-Cas9, by contrast, have drastically lowered costs of entry to gene editing, and whether you want to cure cancer or create biological weapons of mass destruction, the necessary technology might soon be available for tens of thousands of dollars rather than billions. The consequences of that, with the cost of editing the genetic material of both ourselves and other species falling ever closer to zero, are difficult to overstate.

Yet we are starting to catch glimpses of what that future might look like. In early 2017 the US Food and Drug Administration was contacted by David Ishee, a kennel operator based in Mississippi with a passion for biohacking. Ishee had recently been developing his skills with CRISPR-Cas9, conducting personal experiments in his garden laboratory. He hoped to use the technique to eliminate an inherited condition common to Dalmatians called hyperuricemia, which can cause gout, and had sent the FDA an outline of his plans. Having presumed agency approval was a mere formality, Ishee was surprised when he received no response.

On January 18 it became clear why, as the FDA released a proposal to regulate cattle, pigs, dogs and other animals modified with gene-editing tools, including CRISPR-Cas9. A previously ambiguous area at the interface of DIY culture and high-value technology would now require federal approval and be subject to significant government oversight.

That came as a blow to Ishee, who told one outlet that it would be 'easier to teach dog breeders CRISPR than ... why pure breeding is a bad thing'. His view was that the genetic material of pedigree dogs is in no way 'natural' to begin with, and that CRISPR offered a means of correcting biological errors which were the result of human intervention.

The FDA proposed treating the edited portion of an animal's genome as equivalent to a veterinary drug. So just like a new pill, edited animals can't be sold, or even given away. And, just as importantly, it is likely edited genomes may be subject to intellectual property rights and patent. Imagine the battle over Napster, the file-sharing P2P network at the turn of the millennium, and now apply it to biology. Even if information does want to be free – or at least wants to be consistently cheaper over time – that doesn't matter when there are incumbent business and profit models to protect.

While there are justified safety concerns which need to be managed and regulated, turning edited DNA – including our own – into a commodity exclusively for profit, is entirely consistent with the logic of capitalism. As we have seen elsewhere, artificial scarcity has to be imposed in order to create a market – otherwise nobody can make a profit. Ishee's comments in response to the announcement perhaps offer a sign, however, of what direct action might look like as the Third Disruption accelerates: 'I feel like maybe the best thing is to just go ahead and produce the healthy animals and then just tell people ... we cured this disease, but the FDA won't let us.'

Welcome to Elysium

Parallels can be drawn between David Ishee and his biohacking efforts in modern-day Mississippi and the film *Elysium*, set in 2154. In the latter, Earth has been ravaged by climate change and what appears to be a breakdown in the formal economy. As a result, the wealthy have departed for an off-world colony named Elysium – a giant space-habitat orbiting the Earth. The difference in quality of life between its inhabitants and those left behind could not be more striking.

One of the many benefits bestowed on Elysians is access to its Med-Bays, machines that can cure disease, seemingly reverse ageing and regenerate entire body parts. The central plot of the film revolves around Max Da Costa – a former car thief living among the ruins of Los Angeles – and his efforts to access a Med-Bay after being exposed to lethal amounts of radiation. Max's quest is mirrored by the efforts of his childhood friend Frey, as she pursues a cure for her young daughter dying from Leukaemia. The only problem is the use of Med-Bays are exclusively limited to citizens of Elysium, and they don't function with anyone else. That means the only hope for Max and Frey's daughter is to change the operating system of the entire habitat, making its technology available to outsiders like them.

The film culminates with a hacker named Spider uploading a program from Max's brain to reboot Elysium's operating system and extend citizenship to those on Earth. Shortly after that is completed, robots depart to tend to the sick and dying. Rather than an act of charity they are simply upholding their protocol: of caring for Elysians.

While it might not be immediately obvious, Elysium is a film about rights. The tensions between universal human rights and the foreclosed rights of the citizen; between the right to private property and the right to access public forms of healthcare. For most people, intuitively anyway, the right to life for some eclipses the 'right' to unimaginable wealth for others. This is why the final scene of the film is a happy one, despite Max making the ultimate sacrifice.

So as well as being a story about a plausible future for humanity, Elysium also offers a parable for how the Third Disruption might develop. Its meaning is obvious: there is more than enough technology for everyone on Earth to live healthy, happy, fulfilling lives. What stands in the way isn't the inevitable scarcity of nature, but the artificial scarcity of market rationing and ensuring that everything, at all costs, is produced for profit.

This dissonance will only become more grating over time, especially given the medical technologies identified above. That's why we will need to change the operating system of our society too.

Perhaps we are already seeing the world that *Elysium* depicts. In December 2015 SpaceX landed its Falcon 9 rocket, making it the first reusable booster to successfully enter orbital space and return for a second flight. This was a signal moment in the history of space technology, with reusable rockets of critical importance in making the industry commercially viable.

A few months earlier, in September, images of a dead child on a Turkish beach made headlines around the world. Alan Kurdi had been born three years earlier in Kobani, a city in Syrian Kurdistan close to the Turkish border and a focal point in that country's civil war. Having fled their home during a sustained siege by ISIS, Kurdi's family returned there that January only to leave a few months later when fighting started once more. Like many of their compatriots Kurdi's family sought refuge in Europe, and in the early hours of 2 September Alan boarded an illegal boat set for the Greek island of Kos with his brother and parents. Within minutes the vessel capsized. At 6:30 AM Kurdi's body was found by locals in Bodrum. Within days his corpse, along with that of his mother Rehana and brother Ghalib, were returned to Kobani for burial.

The family of Alan Kurdi, like thousands in the summer of 2015, sought to enter Europe in search of the sanctuary, dignity and opportunity they deserved as human beings. While the countries of Western Europe might not have the medical technologies of Elysium, the reusable rockets which were successfully piloted within months of Kurdi's death make for an all-too-obvious analogue. A world which will soon have the technology to sequence the genome of every organism on Earth also permits thousands to drown in the Mediterranean every year.

While gene therapies and daily genome sequencing aren't Med-Bays, they do have the potential to seriously disrupt the provision of healthcare, potentially eliminating conditions which debilitate or kill millions of people a year. More importantly these technologies, underpinned by exponential improvements and tendencies to extreme supply, not only allow us to keep pace with the unique health challenges presented by societal ageing, but even surpass them. While we are often told we can't afford to maintain ever-older societies, and that socialised forms of healthcare are particularly unsustainable, it is the opposite which is true. Socialised forms of healthcare, as study after study show, are more efficient as well as being more equitable. It is only by keeping and expanding them, while integrating these new technologies, that society can progress. This fundamental truth, combined with healthcare that increasingly resembles an information good, has implications far more profound than free encyclopaedias or films. It could even spell the end of age-related and inherited illness altogether.

The alternative? That new forms of biological inequality

map onto extant economic ones as the wealthy alter their off-springs' DNA to make them superior to the rest of us in every way, undermining the basis for modern human rights — that all humans are created equal.

8

Food Without Animals:
Post-Scarcity in Sustenance

Cattle are very inefficient animals in converting vegetable proteins into animal proteins. We actually lose a lot of food by giving it to animals as an intermediate.

Mark Post, inventor of cultured meat

We figured out how life really works and now we don't need to cause death to create food.

Just Food Promotional Video

Food, Surplus and Disruptions

The First Disruption was a revolution in food more than anything else. While prior to it our ancestors possessed simple technologies such as fire and stone tools, before the arrival of agriculture their impact was limited. As a result, any census of human life even as recently as 12,000 years ago, would have shown little more than 5 million people covering the entire planet – equivalent to the population of modern-day Ireland.

Everything began to change as cultivating crops and breed-ing livestock enabled larger, more complex forms of society. No longer were our forebears subject to the whim of other predators, famine or natural disaster. Now they could prepare for the future, creating surplus during times of plenty as well as tools and forms of infrastructure to progressively expand their newly acquired abundance.

Given the frequency of scare stories surrounding geneti-cally modified foods as embodying the worst aspects of modern technology, it is ironic that many staples we now take for granted were only developed through genetic modification during this period. Carrots, initially harvested in Afghanistan eleven thousand years ago, were once purple and white, while bananas – now the world's favourite fruit – are sterile and incapable of setting seed, and have been ever since our ances-tors began to cultivate them following the last Ice Age. While critics are right to say that a technological fix isn't, in isolation, sufficient to resolve issues of ecological degradation and food scarcity, in a very meaningful sense technology is precisely what underpinned the success of our species in the first place.

A Stretching World

But while the story of humanity's rise is built on agriculture, and its unique ability to reprogramme the gifts of nature, it now appears that such genius has found the natural limits of our planet. These limits are more obvious than ever and are expressed in a number of ways. The most striking is a sixth mass extinction event, in which one in four mammals is set to vanish. At the same time 90 per cent of the largest fish in our oceans have disappeared, the glaciers that provide drinking water for billions are starting to run dry, and agricultural soils are becoming increasingly salty – degraded by the excesses of industrial farming. In short, the treasures of our planet – mineral, animal and plant – are being decimated, and the rate of their demise is only accelerating.

The reason why is simple. At present humanity consumes the resources of 1.6 Earths every year, despite the fact that more than 2 billion people survive on less than 2,000 calories a day. That would appear to suggest there are too many of us. If so, the last thing we'd want would be for the world's poor to enjoy lifestyles similar to those of the more affluent countries. This poses a problem for anyone who wishes to address issues of global inequality and poverty, because any meaningful improvement regarding them would seemingly exacerbate environmental breakdown.

But it doesn't end there. The Earth's human population is expected to rise by a further 2 billion people ahead of 2050, and in order to provide all 9.6 billion of us a balanced diet, the UN's Food and Agriculture Organisation believes food production would have to increase by 70 per cent. In other words, by the middle of this century humanity would need the resources of more than two planet Earths simply for everyone to enjoy a decent standard of living.

Even that might be optimistic, however. Were everyone to enjoy the same diet as the average American does right now, consuming approximately 3,700 calories every day, we would need the resources of an additional five Earths within a generation. Even if you wanted today's United States to be a template for global development, from the perspective of bio-capacity that isn't remotely possible.

And when you integrate reasonable forecasts about the impact of climate change for agriculture the picture gets even worse. A 2009 report predicted that warming of three degrees would mean a 50 per cent reduction in wheat yields in South Asia between 2000 and 2050, along with a 17 per cent reduction in rice and six per cent in maize. That in a region with three of the eight most populous countries in the world – India, Pakistan and Bangladesh – all of which are set to see their respective populations rise further over the coming years. Furthermore the glaciers which feed the great rivers of the Indian subcontinent, the Brahmaputra, the Ganges and the Indus, which provide drinking water to hundreds of millions, are starting to disappear.

That same study forecast a decline in East Asian rice production by 20 per cent and wheat by 16 per cent. In sub-Saharan Africa, whose population is anticipated to double between now and 2050, rice yields would decline by 14 and wheat by 22 per cent. For the Middle East, like Africa particularly subject to the twin challenges of increased water scarcity and rapidly rising populations, it is even worse, with rice yields declining by 30 per cent, maize by 47 per cent and wheat by 20 per cent.

That isn't to say the comparatively wealthier countries of the Global North will remain unaffected, however. Within a low warming scenario, forecasts suggest the US would see corn and soy yields fall by 30 and 46 per cent respectively. Given the country is currently the world's leading exporter of grains, that would spell disaster not only at home but for the world market. Even if other countries such as Russia and Canada stepped up to become agricultural powerhouses, this might only serve to increase the possibility of resource conflicts with their more militarily powerful neighbours.

Forget post-scarcity. Between rising populations, climate change, a dearth of fresh water and stretched bio-capacity, just avoiding widespread famine by the middle of this century would represent an astonishing achievement. So how exactly can our planet sustainably feed a world of 9.6 billion people?

~

Under current models of food production, the answer largely depends on the kind of diet that is adopted. Over a year, the average American consumes 800 kilograms of grain in the form of food and secondary animal feed. Were that to become the global average then the present level of grain production, slightly above 2 billion metric tonnes, would only support a global population of 2.5 billion. By contrast if the average was in line with the Mediterranean diet, where each person consumes around 400 kilograms of grain a year, the earth could maintain a population double that. Finally, if all of us ate – directly and indirectly – the same quantity of grains as the average Indian, then present methods of food production could sustain a planetary population of 10 billion, more or less where we'll be by the closing decades of this century.

Put bluntly it is the meat and dairy consumption typical to diets of the Global North which have us living beyond our ecological means. Current levels of food production could even meet demand for 2050, but it would require a typical diet almost absent of animal protein.

There is at least some good news, however. While the Earth's human population has exploded since the dawn of the Second Disruption, it is likely to peak at 10 billion this century – thereafter either falling or remaining static. From the perspective of mouths to feed that means it won't look that different from today – an extra 3 billion people – which is what the world has added since 1974. Indeed, it is rising expectations in diet, combined with declining crop yields as a result of climate change, which represent the biggest hurdles in eliminating world hunger.

Claims about rising populations and the natural limits of the Earth are nothing new. Indeed Thomas Malthus, one of the most important thinkers in the early history of political economy, was obsessed by the issue. In his 1798 polemic *An Essay on the Principle of Population*, he observed how any increase in food production led to a growth in population rather than an improvement in the average standard of living. His resulting conclusion was stark. 'The power of population is so superior to the power of the earth to produce subsistence for man that premature death must in some shape or other visit the human race.'

Malthus was far from unique in such reasoning. William Jevons, an English economist writing in the 1860s, noted how more efficient steam engines counter-intuitively meant more coal was consumed rather than less – an observation since referred to as the 'Jevons Paradox'. Between Malthus and Jevons the verdict appeared to be the same: humanity's ingenuity, as vast as it is, can never hope to keep pace with its voracious appetites.

Yet the story of agriculture over the second half of the twentieth century tells us otherwise. While feeding a world of 9 billion might seem impossible, especially so within the broader context of the five crises, the most important achievement of the last sixty years suggests it can be done. Its name? The Green Revolution.

Food as Information: The Green Revolution

At present the amount of land given over to agriculture is around 37.5 per cent of the world's land area – which is more or less the same as it was in the late 1970s. Yet our planet now supports an extra 3 billion people, while average calorie consumption has increased and food deprivation has fallen. Indeed, in the last two decades alone, the number of people experiencing hunger halved to around 10 per cent of the world's population. All of this was achieved while fewer and fewer people were employed in agriculture.

This suggests there is another way to feed 9 billion people, one that would mean we had more than enough food for everyone, all without the need for rationing or changing eating habits. Indeed, it would make food so abundant that – as with energy, labour and resources – it would become virtually free, with the value emerging more from the informational content than inputs such as land or human effort.

While you may never have heard of him, Norman Borlaug was one of the most important figures of the twentieth century. A year after receiving his PhD in 1942 he assumed an agricultural research position in Mexico where he developed semi-dwarf, high-yield varieties of wheat – a crop the country was failing to produce in sufficient amounts. These modified varieties used most of their energy to grow edible kernels rather than long, inedible stems and had the additional benefit of being disease-resistant. Financed by the UN, various US government agencies and the Rockefeller Foundation, this was the very latest in agronomic research – and more than a decade before we understood how DNA and inheritance actually worked.

Mexican wheat production quickly flourished. By 1956 the country was self-sufficient in the crop, and by 1964 it exported half a million tons of it. In the space of two decades the majority of the country's wheat came from the newer grains bred by Borlaug. But problems with food production extended far beyond Mexico. In a world of nations newly freed of European empires, the spectre of global hunger was more pressing than ever. Economic under-development as a result of colonialism, combined with growing populations and relatively weak state structures, seemed a dangerous mix in an uncertain world.

Which is why in 1961, as India stood on the brink of famine, Borlaug was invited to apply his skills beyond central America. There the region of Punjab had been selected to experiment with recently developed crops created by the new International Rice Research Institute (IRRI). Just as with Mexico, India would subsequently make huge leaps forward as a result of its own programme of plant breeding, irrigation development and use of agrochemicals. Arguably, however, it was the adoption of the IR8 rice variety – a semi-dwarf grain developed by the IRRI – which proved decisive. Findings published in 1968 showed it to yield five tons per hectare without fertiliser, and almost ten tons under optimal conditions – a 900 per cent increase on traditional rice varieties in the country. That same year, the biologist Paul Ehrlich published the best-selling *The Population Bomb* which detailed how famine, particularly in India, would kill hundreds of millions over the following decades. With unremitting certainty, he wrote, 'I don't see how India could possibly feed two hundred million more people by 1980.'

Except it did, and all while life expectancy doubled and a country historically plagued by colonially-imposed famine became the world's leading exporter of rice by the early twenty-first century. Such unexpected success was the legacy of Borlaug, the IRRI and the Green Revolution more generally, the central principle of which was that food is ultimately information.

And, as we know, any information can be reprogrammed.

Completing the Green Revolution

Much of the Green Revolution, which transformed Asian agriculture in particular, involved spreading techniques and infrastructure already common to the industrialised nations.

This included modern irrigation projects, as well as the use of chemical pesticides and synthetic fertiliser. Its primary aspect, however, was the adoption of vastly improved, and genetically modified, crop varieties. That is why wheat yields have tripled since the early 1970s among developing countries – possibly saving a billion lives in the process.

But what if that Green Revolution, which allowed us to feed more people than ever before, and using less labour to do so, was only the beginning? What if, rather than inhabiting an exhausted planet, we had only begun to understand how our mastery of nature could confer almost limitless abundance? If information wants to be free – and the bounty of nature is highly complex arrangements of information – then why should hunger exist at all?

The first Green Revolution seemingly confounded Malthus, Jevons and Ehrlich, confirming that our collective intelligence is sufficient to satisfy our appetites. As with so much in the twentieth century, however, that isn't to say it came without a cost. Fossil fuels were burned like never before, only accelerating climate change, while natural habitats were destroyed, rivers and lakes were poisoned and soil became ever less fertile. The last century may have proven the pessimists wrong, but it still appears we are living on borrowed time. The reprieve was temporary.

No less an issue is the treatment of animals within this ultra-efficient paradigm of farming. The agricultural practices of the modern era may deliver higher amounts of protein, carbohydrate and fat, but in addition to exhausting our planet it also brings immense suffering to sentient life. Millions of male chicks, along with their shells, are macerated alive on conveyor belts because they can't lay eggs, while chickens in battery farms spend their lives in a space the size of an A4 sheet of paper pumped with antibiotics to stop infection. Female cows must calve at least once a year to continually produce milk and are artificially inseminated to do so. A cow would naturally suckle her calf for nine months to a year, but calves born on dairy farms are taken from their mothers within days of being born – a traumatic experience for both animals. Males are of little use to a dairy farmer and more than one hundred thousand bull calves are shot in the UK every year.

Highly automated food production might feed more people than ever, but the sight of such slaughter is something which few would wish to watch or even know about.

Synthetic Meat: Meat without Animals

With the exception of some extraordinary organisms at the bottom of the ocean, almost all life on earth is powered by the sun. Plants and algae feed themselves through a solar-powered chemical reaction called photosynthesis, combining carbon dioxide from the air with water. This is done with chlorophyll, a green pigment which gives these organisms their colour, and is responsible for capturing the sun's energy. The same process occurs with phytoplankton in the oceans, tiny organisms responsible for half the world's oxygen and the basis for nearly all marine life.

These solar-powered life-forms provide the energy for herbivores such as bison, elephants and zooplankton in the wild, and domesticated animals such as sheep and cows. In turn these animals form the basis of the carnivorous diet, whether it be for predators such as large cats, larger fish, or humans and domesticated animals. Humans have generally reared and eaten omnivores and herbivores. In addition to being easier to feed, these creatures also have higher levels of body fat meaning there are more calories to go round.

Nevertheless, compared to a plant-based diet, animals remain energy intensive and inefficient at converting solar energy to food. A Bangladeshi family living off rice, beans, vegetables and fruit can subsist on an acre of land or less. Meanwhile the average American, who consumes 270 pounds of meat a year, could require as much as twenty times that. If you examine the inputs necessary to produce a pound of soy protein compared to animal protein, the latter uses twelve times as much land, thirteen times as much fossil fuels and fifteen times as much water – and soy is a famously inefficient non-meat product.

Nearly a third of the useable surface area of the planet is given over to livestock either directly or indirectly, with animal feed accounting for the majority of global crop production. One study by Cornell University found that while 302 million hectares were given over to livestock in the United States, only 13 million hectares were allocated to vegetables, rice, fruit, potatoes and beans. Such a huge gap shows that animal products are a highly inefficient way of using finite resources to produce food.

What's more, livestock farming contributes to 14 per cent of all human caused greenhouse gas emissions and, according to a 2006 report by the UN, generates greater amounts of CO_2 than cars. Meanwhile 69 per cent of the world's freshwater withdrawals are committed to agriculture, most of which is in meat production, with the average cow consuming 11,000 gallons of water a year. That means the average pound of ground beef requires 440 gallons of water, while a dozen eggs need an astonishing 636 gallons. And all in a world where 3.4 million people die every year from water-related disease.

Most remarkable of all is that after using all this water, energy, land and labour – not to mention the greenhouse gas emissions created as a by-product – we dispense with as much as half of the animal's carcass. A heifer weighing a thousand pounds will, on average, produce 610 pounds of 'hanging weight', with this falling to 430 pounds of retail cuts after the removal of bone and fat. Once you factor in skin and hooves, two years of digestive processes, consciousness, respiration and just moving around, food from a living cow starts to look incredibly wasteful as a means of transforming solar energy into beef and milk.

Given the challenges of climate change, resource scarcity and rising populations, it is clear that the world needs to eat far less meat than it does. Preferably, we would completely eliminate it from our diets. But what about freedom of choice? After all, humans might be better adapted to eating fruit and vegetables, but we are omnivores and animals provide a tasty source of protein. In many countries the consumption of meat is viewed as part of a broader cultural heritage, and regardless of health risks and saving the planet, those kinds of value systems take decades to change, if at all.

Yet as with all the other crises examined so far, there is a solution running parallel with a paradigm which seems so utterly untenable. It turns out we could feed more people better food, save the planet and reduce energy demand, all while virtually ending animal suffering in agriculture. In a certain sense, it represents the culmination of the Green Revolution and food becoming an informational good. Its name is cellular agriculture.

The $325,000 Hamburger

In 2008 a Dutch professor named Mark Post presented the proof of concept for what he called 'cultured meat'. Five years later in a London TV studio, Post and his colleagues ate a burger they had grown in a laboratory using those same principles. Secretly funded by Google's Sergey Brin, the journey from petri dish to plate had cost approximately $325,000 — making theirs the most expensive meal in history. Fortunately, the results were promising, with the consensus being that the patty was 'close to meat but not as juicy'. Here was confirmation that Post's concept worked. The next question was the extent to which it might be refined, scaled up and made cheaper. Much cheaper.

History will likely remember Post as the person who took the field of cellular agriculture to a mass audience. It is unlikely, however, that he will be the one to perfect it given the sheer number of individuals and organisations working in an increasingly crowded field. Cellular agriculture can be understood as an approach which designs new mechanisms to re-create existing foods. While much of the attention so far has been on cultured meat, its possibilities go far wider extending into cheese without cows and yeast that can make vegetables taste like medium rare beef. Think of it, perhaps, as the work of Norman Borlaug meeting the second half of that exponential chessboard.

Underpinned by the same technologies of the Third Disruption, defined by declining costs of information and exponential progress in digital technology, it is no coincidence that cellular agriculture arrived at around the same time as genome sequencing, consumer AI and autonomous vehicles. Ultimately it will mean a world where producing meat, leather, milk and eggs no longer requires animals.

Post's approach is easy to grasp if not to execute. First you remove a small sample of muscle from an animal before isolating stem cell tissue which can be scaled in a bioreactor. You then proceed to warm it while feeding those cells with oxygen, sugar and minerals. After between nine and twenty-one days, the developed cells – which have grown into skeletal muscle – are harvested. At present this approach can't work with all meats, especially those whose composition is highly complex and contains additional fats. It is a different story, however, with fish, shellfish and avian meat, whose lean protein content make them the perfect candidates for early-stage innovation in the field. Indeed initial evidence suggests avian muscle cells may not even need a scaffold to grow like red meat, and could instead be cultured in a vessel-like keg or bioreactor in a manner not dissimilar to brewing beer.

The early meat products will most likely be fish, however. Perhaps it's only fitting that the last animals hunted for food on a mass scale, could be among the first grown synthetically for a consumer market. One player in the field, Finless Foods, believes they can get their product to market as soon as 2019 by developing synthetic fish fillets 'in a brewery-like environment'. The most likely candidate is the much-valued bluefin tuna, a fish the company's CEO Mike Selden believes can be price competitive before 2020.

Even more impressive than the original concept behind the technology are improvements in price performance since. While Post's original hamburger cost $325,000 to create in 2013, just three years later US-based Memphis Meats produced the first cultured meatball for $1000. While that might sound like a lot, it represented a significant fall in price, with a quarter-pounder of meat now costing less than 2 per cent of Post's original patty. But it didn't stop there: a year earlier Post, now at Mosa Meats, had already claimed the process he initially pioneered could produce beef in a laboratory for $80 a kilo, meaning that a burger using cultured meat could cost as little as $12 – a more than 99 per cent fall in cost from just four years earlier. And all in the absence of truly industrial-scale production.

That isn't to say there aren't major hurdles to commercially viable steaks that don't require cows. For one thing the material in which the stem cells currently grow is foetal calf serum. Using animal products to feed 'synthetic' animal tissue defeats the whole point, although those at the forefront of the industry claim a vegan alternative isn't far away.

The other major issue is energy – specifically for synthetic mammal meat like pork, beef and chicken. While synthetic seafood will be able to grow at room temperature, mammal meats need something close to the temperature of our bodies. So while any shift to synthetic meat could offer major savings in land use, greenhouse gas emissions, labour and water, the amount of energy consumed could be higher. With the trends already outlined around renewable energy and heat conservation, however, this is a relatively small price to pay.

Given the ecological overhead of contemporary meat production – as well as its intense demand for scarce resources – synthetic meat could offer a paradigm shift. Uma Valeti, CEO of Memphis Meats, thinks synthetic products will take most of the market but not all of it, specifying, 'We are not out to end all forms of animal agriculture. We're opposed to factory farms, not family farms. But family farms can only supply a tiny fraction of the world's demand for meat.'

Mike Selden, CEO of Finless Foods, disagrees, however, placing greater emphasis on animal rights and welfare. 'We've moved past needing to kill animals and ruin the environment for food; we can do much better with the technology that we have.' Regardless of who is right, the advantages of synthetic meat are in keeping with tendencies to extreme supply. More than simply meeting the challenges of climate change and a growing population, this technology permits abundance like never before. Just imagine it, cheap, healthy, delicious meat with no animal suffering, no antibiotics and no hygiene concerns.

While synthetic meat is the most prominent aspect of cellular agriculture and has already attracted vast amounts of venture capital, it is also the most technically difficult to perfect. What is more, while certain kinds of meat like fish, ground beef and chicken breast could soon be commercially scalable, specific cuts like ribs, a T-bone steak, or even fatty bacon, will prove far harder to replicate. The breakthrough will likely come from the same process used to grow muscle tissue being applied to fats and then using a 3-D printer to 'print' steaks, bacon rashers or even a leg of lamb.

By the early 2020s we will start to see these products for sale – indeed Just Food launched its first chicken nugget product at the end of 2018. Initially expensive they will be the preserve of environmentally conscious and affluent consumers who prize ethical consumption over flavour. But as the decade progresses that will change with synthetic meat becoming more and more common – especially where ground, seasoned meat is used like in meatballs, hamburgers and hot dogs.

Were synthetic meat to completely replace present forms of meat production, it would put even the achievements of the Green Revolution in the shade. The savings in land, water and human labour would be immense, as would the reduction in emissions of methane and CO_2, with some estimates claiming that synthetic meat could require 90 per cent less land and water then current meat production. A 2011 report conducted by the Universities of Amsterdam and Oxford concluded that cultured meat could potentially require 45 per cent less energy, 99 per cent less land, and 96 per cent less water than conventional meat, not to mention leading to 96 per cent fewer greenhouse gas emissions. That same report stated that if the US switched to synthetic beef, the likely reduction in greenhouse gas emissions would be equivalent to taking 23 million cars off the country's roads, with the substitution of a single cultured meat burger for the 'real thing' saving water equivalent to over fifty showers.

With meat and dairy consumption set to double between 2000 and 2050, synthetic meat wouldn't just be a nice thing to have – it will prove critical in meeting the rising demands of people around the world. Given what has happened to production costs in the decade since the field was first conceptualised, it seems likely that synthetic meat won't just compete on price with animal meat but will, in the not too distant future, be far cheaper. All this while alleviating suffering and reducing our use of otherwise finite resources. Post's personal view is that synthetic meat will be competitive on price within twenty years. The truth is that the power of the experience curve could mean it's even sooner.

Meat from Vegetables

Cellular agriculture extends beyond just synthetic meat, however. Indeed, farming minced meat, fillets and breasts from stem cells remains incredibly time-consuming – at least for now – and while these products could be mainstream within a generation, for some that isn't soon enough. Which is why Impossible Foods have chosen a different approach in trying to create vegan products that are indistinguishable from meat. But rather than 'grow' meat proteins, they think they can do that by making non-meat proteins more closely resemble those found in animals.

The science behind their model, which for now focuses on their flagship 'Impossible Burger', is far simpler than creating animal meat minus the animal. Nevertheless, it remains in the ambit of cellular agriculture because the intention is to create new biological mechanisms to produce existing foods. While the approach favoured by the likes of Mark Post is to create synthetic meat by eliminating the animal from a set of biological processes, Impossible Foods want to go even further and just use vegetables. While that might sound outlandish perhaps it shouldn't. After all, from a biohacker's perspective a cow is just a chemical reaction that converts feed and oxygen into beef.

Part of the allure in opting for such a model is that much of nature's abundance remains unknown. Collectively comprising 8 billion proteins, 108 million fats and 4 million carbohydrates, the composition of most of the world's 353,000 plant species remains little understood. From the perspective of Impossible Foods these are nothing less than nature's tools in eliminating processed sugar, salt and – yes – even meat from our diets.

Leading this revolution in re-engineering our food is 'heme', the secret ingredient in the Impossible Burger. Heme is the molecule that gives blood its colour and helps carry oxygen in living organisms, but more importantly for Impossible it accounts for the rich, iron-like taste we associate with juicy medium-rare beef.

While heme is abundant in animal muscle tissue it can also be found elsewhere in nature, particularly nitrogen-fixing plants and legumes. The only problem is that if you wanted to substitute plant sources for animal ones you would need approximately an acre of soybeans to yield a single kilogram of soy leghaemoglobin. That's where Impossible Foods have found a solution. They took genes that code for the protein and inserted them into a species of yeast called *Pichia pastoris* which they then fed with sugars and minerals, prompting it to grow and replicate. This, again, is 'growing' food – in this case a specific ingredient – in a manner not dissimilar to making beer.

For an Impossible Burger, heme is the decisive element adding the taste, texture and smell of 'meat'. Other than that, the burger merely substitutes animal fats and proteins for vegetable ones such as wheat, coconut oil and potatoes. While the resulting meal isn't a real burger in the sense that one made from synthetic meat is, the ambition is to eventually create burgers – as well as other foods – indistinguishable from their carnal counterparts. And while synthetic meat might be price competitive in a generation, products from companies like Impossible Foods are already available, with the company now producing 1 million pounds of ground 'plant meat' each month. So far investors have thrown almost $275 million at Impossible Foods, but when you consider the size of the global meat market is more than $1 trillion – and growing rapidly despite the constraints of our planet – that seems a prudent investment.

More than Meat

Whether its culturing meat or genetically modifying yeast to create new ingredients, the ambitions of cellular agriculture aren't limited to creating meat without animals. Indeed, the principles are more easily adopted with other foods such as milk, egg whites and even wine.

At present milk appears to be the easiest one of all, and given it is such an important ingredient in a range of animal products – from cream to butter, yoghurt and cheese – an effective substitute would have a massive impact. What's more, hundreds of millions of people are lactose intolerant or prefer not to consume dairy for ethical reasons, making milk an obvious place to start for anyone wishing to be involved in cellular agriculture. Sure, there are plenty of nut and soy milks out there, but none of them taste the same and, more importantly, they can't keep pace with rising global demand.

Perfect Day Foods are one of the first companies who think they can meet the challenge of making cow milk without cows. To do so the company's co-founders, both trained in biomedical engineering, obtained a particular strain of yeast from the US Department of Agriculture and inserted a cow's DNA sequence into it – much like how Impossible Foods did for heme. They then fermented the yeast with sugar, again akin to brewing beer, and made 'real' milk proteins with both casein and whey. These were then combined with plant-based fats and nutrients to produce lactose-free milk. Essentially this is the same process of fermentation as in a cow's four stomachs, except there is no energy being expended on the rest of the animal, no unwanted by-products like methane and carbon dioxide, and land and water consumption is significantly lower.

Then there's eggs. Egg white substitutes are nothing new – indeed one of the most commercially successful vegan products in recent years is the mayonnaise substitute Just. In a manner reminiscent of the Impossible Foods burger, Just Foods examined numerous plant sources that possessed the emulsifying properties of egg whites to make mayonnaise. After examining eleven plant ingredients as a potential replacement they settled on a specific variety of Canadian yellow field pea – a type of split pea which possesses precisely the right properties and required no genetic modification.

But while that is impressive, it still leaves the hundreds of other recipes that need eggs, not to mention their use in omelettes, baking or just cooked plain. Which is where Clara Foods come in. They have developed a way to precisely replicate egg whites without a single chicken. Their process, unsurprisingly, starts with a genetically modified strain of yeast used to 'grow' egg whites and all twelve of its proteins. The potential benefits are immediately obvious: cheaper eggs with no risk of salmonella or avian flu and no need for antibiotics. In addition, they are more sustainable, with far lower greenhouse gas emissions and, again, less land and water being required. The science behind it is promising and, with the ambition of going to market with their synthetic egg whites by 2020, Clara Foods may play a major role in ending the welfare issues associated with battery egg production – all while leading to a healthier, cheaper product.

That's all very well, but what about the egg yolks needed for things like making pasta and omelettes? Clara Foods intend to produce a similar product there as well, but until then Just will have the field to themselves after releasing their 'Just Scramble' scrambled eggs, made from a mung bean extract, in the summer of 2018.

Champagne Socialism

Cellular agriculture isn't limited to the necessities of life. Indeed, things begin to get really interesting with wine, which unlike most food and drink, has a highly specific taste profile endowing each bottle with a distinctive status and value. And while the process in potentially replicating wine is different to the foods examined above, that means it – perhaps more than any other food or drink – is liable to becoming an information good.

The only barrier, until now, has been our inability to collect or replicate the necessary information. If we could, then a vintage magnum would start to resemble an MP3.

The uniqueness of each grape, terroir and year is part of the romance surrounding wine. To the refined palate, a 1990 Château Margaux is an entirely different drink than the reduced bottle of claret at the supermarket. From a commercial perspective this makes wine a great place to start for biotechnology companies, because it is highly popular but has multiple price points. If what we think about economic rationality is even remotely correct, the right incentives exist for wine to be at the forefront of the synthetic food revolution.

That explains why a company called Endless West (previously Ava Winery) have jumped into the field with both feet. Not only do they think they can re-create wine without grapes, or fermentation, but that ultimately they will be able to replicate the precise flavour of particular grape varieties, soils and vintages. How they plan to do that is through molecular assembly, adopting a 'scan and print' approach in cataloguing existing wines, before recreating them with a precise mix of amino acids, glycerin, sugars and ethanol. The end product could be a classic bottle at a massively discounted price – and they have already tried replicating a 1992 Dom Pérignon (though it was never released).

But wine has a highly complex flavour profile so, in a pivot to whiskey, they recently launched Glyph – what they refer to as the world's first 'molecular spirit'. If Endless West's approach works it would, like so much else in the context of the Third Disruption, make previously high-value alcohol an informational good. Overnight the most precious of bottles, whose value is a function of their scarcity, would be technically subject to infinite replication. What's more this process would require far less land, water and labour – indeed it could very likely be entirely automated. It's ironic that the perennial dismissal of left-wing radicals as indulging in 'champagne socialism' might be a fitting description of our not-too-distant future.

For now the wines are easily distinguishable from the real thing, with the brand's Moscato described by one reviewer as exhibiting a 'plastic aroma and taste' and reeking 'with artificiality'. Their whiskey is a different story, however, with the *Washington Post* describing how it had touches of liquorice and apple and tasted better than Pappy Van Winkle's Twenty-Year-Old Family Reserve, one of the world's most-prized bourbons.

Besides the huge savings in labour, time, energy, land and water, synthetic biology will underpin a historic relocation of food production. Synthetic meat, which needs no sunlight, would appear to be a perfect candidate for vertical, urban farming, while the obvious savings with land come to fundamentally alter our relationship with nature.

This could have a number of benefits including the re-wilding of vast wildernesses lost to deforestation and the Industrial Revolution – certainly of major use as carbon sinks in trying to mitigate climate change. Meanwhile, the end of global food distribution, at least in its present form, would avert colossal amounts of waste. At present the average ingredient in an American meal travels 1,550 miles before consumption, while 70 per cent of a food's final retail price comes from transportation, storage and handling. In a society emphasising energy abundance through efficiency as much as extreme supply, the idea that 127 calories of fuel would be used to fly a calorie of iceberg lettuce from the US to the UK, as is presently the case, will be rightly viewed as absurd.

Indeed, just like gene editing it's possible that DIY cultures will accompany the rise of hyper-local production with our ever-expanding leisure time given over to home-brewing rib-eye steaks and Gruyère cheese as much as beer or cider.

III.
Paradise Found

Invention, it must be humbly admitted, does not consist in creating out of void, but out of chaos.

Mary Shelley

With the abolition of private property, then, we shall have true, beautiful, healthy Individualism. Nobody will waste his life in accumulating things, and the symbols for things. One will live. To live is the rarest thing in the world.

Oscar Wilde

9
Popular Support: Luxury Populism

We want everything.

Nanni Balestrini

Against Elite Technocracy

The technologies of the Third Disruption are already creating a new set of dispositions towards the world. As a result, every aspect of social life, from ownership to work and even scarcity is being transformed.

From that observation emerges several questions: How can these dispositions be turned into political power? How can the distance between the future we thought was on offer, and the disappointment of the present, be breached? How do we translate seemingly individual, personal problems into a bold and emphatic 'we'?

The answer to all three enquiries begins with an admission. While the tendency to extreme supply means everything will become permanently cheaper — from food to transport and clothing — all as a result of each factor of production falling in price thanks to the central role of information, in the absence of an appropriate politics this will only lead to novel forms of profiteering. Marx expressed this perfectly when he wrote, 'The most developed machinery thus forces the worker to work longer than the savage does, or than he himself did with the simplest, crudest tools.'

In response to that admission, an assertion: any successful politics that seeks to submit the possibilities of the Third Disruption to the needs of people rather than profit must be populist. If not, it is certain to fail. Capitalist realism is simply too adaptable for a radical politics of management and technocracy, meaning any rupture must be understandable to most people in an idiom that they readily understand. What is more, the wider social benefits of the shift to Fully Automated Luxury Communism must be seen as running parallel to flourishing on a personal scale, rather than a sacrifice to some greater good. This is the politics of the self-help guru – be precisely who you want to be – embedded within a broader programme for political change. You can only live your best life under FALC and nothing else, so fight for it and refuse the yoke of an economic system which belongs in the past.

Populism is a politics that refuses to recognise the prevailing common sense in managing the economy. Consequently a portion of its critics, those most seduced by capitalist realism, attack it from the incorrect assumption that there is no alternative to neoliberalism. As the status quo is imperilled by the five crises, as well as the long fallout from 2008, such defences will increasingly take place through appeals to anti-utopianism rather than anything positive or propositional. Thus even standard-bearers for the establishment might concede that living standards are getting worse, or that society is going backwards by many measures, but at least, they will respond, we aren't in 1990s Rwanda and aren't medieval serfs. Such a position signifies the death of the very idea of the future, with enlightenment and progress – formerly ideological pillars of liberal capitalism – exchanged for a vision of the good society where decline is marginally slower than it might otherwise be.

Others, who may agree about the scale and even urgent necessity of change, will contend that such a radical path should only be pursued by a narrow technocratic elite. Such an impulse is understandable if not excusable; or the suspicion that democracy unleashes 'the mob' is as old as the idea itself. What is more, a superficial changing of the guard exclusively at the level of policy-making is easier to envisage than building a mass political movement – and far simpler to execute as a strategy. Yet the truth is any social settlement imposed without mass consent, particularly given the turbulent energies unleashed by the Third Disruption, simply won't endure.

Which is why for the kind of change required, and for it to last in a world increasingly at odds with the received wisdom of the past, a populist politics is necessary. One that blends culture and government with ideas of personal and social renewal. One that, to borrow a term, invents the future. Anything less will fall short.

A populist politics is one that calls upon, and claims to represent, 'the people'. While this category does not exist as a permanent and immutable entity, what does prevail are parameters that elevate certain kinds of assembly, social trait or capacity. That is why the 'ethnic people' is defined by the community of blood and land; the 'democratic people' by the shared act of forging legitimate authority through elections; and the 'ignorant people' by a benevolent elite who generously keeps them at bay or defends them from themselves. The very essence of populism is to determine who 'the people' really are, rendering visible – and powerful – those elements otherwise framed as too incompetent, dangerous or docile to transform society.

Just as was the case with the Second Disruption in early nineteenth-century Europe, populism is the only way to manage the kind of transformation we are set to confront. Then, making sense of a changing world was enacted through new forms of togetherness: nationalism both liberal and authoritarian, imperialism, racism and socialism. The present juncture demands something similar, asking us to create a collective politics that goes beyond scarcity, work and the narrow forms of selfhood and identity offered by neoliberalism. The notion that a ruling class can manage such transition – for better or worse – within such civilisational rift isn't just wrong, it's absurd. What is more if new, appropriate forms of togetherness are not created, those authoritarianisms concocted by previous generations will return.

The Red and the Green

This 'luxury' populism must be both red and green. Red because it places the energies of the Third Disruption at the service of humanity – in the process enhancing personal freedom like never before. Green because it knows climate change is inevitable and that going beyond fossil fuels is a matter of critical urgency. What is more, rather than reducing our quality of life, it grasps how the transition to renewable energy offers a bridge to energy abundance – permitting more prosperous societies than previously possible under the petty limits of fossil fuels.

A green politics of ecology without a red politics of shared wealth will fail to command popular support. Conversely, the promise of red plenty based on fossil fuels and resource scarcity will fall victim to climate breakdown, leaving the world's poor exposed to devastation like never before. Which is why the only politics fit to fight climate change is the demand for FALC – driven by the impulse to lead fuller, expanded lives, not diminished ones.

To the green movement of the twentieth century this is heretical. Yet it is they who, for too long, unwisely echoed the claim that 'small is beautiful' and that the only way to save our planet was to retreat from modernity itself. FALC rallies against that command, distinguishing consumption under fossil capitalism – with its commuting, ubiquitous advertising, bullshit jobs and built-in obsolescence – from pursuing the good life under conditions of extreme supply. Under FALC we will see more of the world than ever before, eat varieties of food we have never heard of, and lead lives equivalent – if we so wish – to those of today's billionaires. Luxury will pervade everything as society based on waged work becomes as much a relic of history as the feudal peasant and medieval knight.

More than the vacuous nihilism of today's ultra-rich, whose ascent beyond scarcity finds its pathetic expression in conspicuous consumption, the process of building FALC will not only bequeath us the resources needed to make us happy, but also a sense of common purpose.

What is more, luxury populism rejects the folk politics of ethical consumption and the sphere of 'the local' as inherently virtuous. The extent of the solutions needed to address the five crises are planetary, and while action will often be close to home – as the following chapters make clear – acknowledging the historic and global scale of any response is critical. Our ambitions must be Promethean because our technology is already making us gods – so we might as well get good at it.

Nevertheless, space must remain for 'grassroots' campaigns which advance the post-scarcity alternative while attacking a broken status quo. Campaigns around divestment from fossil fuels offer one example of how that will work. Rather than calling for climate justice through appeals to turn down the volume on modernity here, criticism of fossil fuels is situated within the broader frame that they are an obstacle to yet higher standards of living. In comparison to solar and wind, hydrocarbons are as unsuitable to the needs of our century as burning whale fat for light was for the last. Digging up and burning mineral deposits for energy is so last century.

The same approach is needed in resisting extraction of shale gas, the most glaring example of the myopia of 'scarcism' amid the final embers of the Second Disruption. While one part of that is to continue pursuing outright bans, like those already in place in France, Germany and New York, this must be done alongside the demand for something better. Here advocates must clamour for the alternative with and alongside communities targeted for fracking, demanding indigenous rights, local democracy and radical land reform along with calls for an end to drilling. In this respect movements in Alaska, Canada and Australia already serve as stunning examples, not to mention the case of Balcombe, a tiny village in Sussex, where a coalition of campaigners and local residents opposed plans for fracking while demanding the alternative of community-owned solar power. The call for clean energy must become synonymous not only with the expectation of permanently falling costs but also common ownership. Prosperity, democracy and the commons as not only connected, but mutually constitutive.

As well as advancing a red–green politics which revives ideals of progress and common plenty, this new populism will also be one of luxury. FALC, unlike the world of actually existing neoliberalism, will not demand constant sacrifices on the altar of profit and growth. Whether it's 'paying down the debt for future generations', as our politicians are so keen to repeat, or growth and rising wages always coming 'next year', it's becoming ever clearer that the good times aren't coming back. What remains absent, however, is a language able to articulate that which is both accessible and emotionally resonant.

Because behind such entreaties – whether from Erdoğan, Trump, Theresa May or the European Central Bank – is an esoteric caste of administrators that nobody else can quite understand. Their language of mathematical economics resembles the high Latin of Europe's priests as they explained the nature of things to illiterate peasants who could never hope to understand. To the Ten Commandments all they add is that economic growth – of any kind – is good, while the pious many must uphold the faith by working harder and spending more than ever.

This demand for constant offerings from taxpayers, hard-working families or 'strivers', all while living standards stagnate, means we are now experiencing what Eastern Bloc socialism endured after the 1970s. Two conspicuous hallmarks of that era similarly characterise our present: falling economic growth and crumbling ideological hegemony. The words of the priests increasingly fall on deaf ears, meaning many now turn to other – often older – faiths to make sense of the seemingly absurd.

Thus the return of 'the people' as the main political actor is inevitable, whether as the rabble who patrician elites defend from their own desires, the *Volk* grounded in land, blood and soil, as witnessed in the revival of the far right, or the masses as a potentially transformative subject which makes history. Many increasingly grasp that the problems we face are large and unprecedented, and they intuitively understand the necessary solutions must be of a similar scale. So given the possibilities of the Third Disruption, promise them what they deserve – promise everything.

Everything against the emptiness of a system in breakdown, with its call to toil for even less than you already have. Everything against the farce of identities which no longer make sense or were myths of little initial purpose. Everything, that is, except the demand of luxury for all. The offer to be who you want, rather than your life being shaped by forces beyond your control.

When we have scaled that summit and surpassed scarcity, having turned the dividend of the Third Disruption to the needs of us all, even the least compassionate will reflect on today's world with regret and pity. Regret at so much lost potential, all the stories never written and lives which might have been so much more. And pity, particularly for those who believed a regime of enforced scarcity made them better than anyone else.

This Is Not 1917

FALC is not the communism of the early twentieth century, nor will it be delivered by storming the Winter Palace. The reason why is that, until the opening decades of the Third Disruption, communism was as impossible as surplus before the First Disruption or electricity before the Second. Instead it was socialism, still defined by scarcity and jobs, which became the North Star for hope across the world.

The technologies needed to deliver a post-scarcity, post-work society – centred around renewable energy, automation and information – were absent in the Russian Empire, or indeed anywhere else until the late 1960s. Indeed, amid efforts to catch up with the more advanced capitalist economies of Europe and America, the Bolsheviks became students of the Taylorist science of productivity, applying themselves to the task of subordinating human time to economic production with ever-greater efficiency. In truth, they had little alternative.

It turns out that Marx's early suspicion that the countries set to lead the revolution would be those at the cutting edge of capitalist modernity was right. Only now we know that means technology as much as politics, the Third Disruption as necessary a precursor as class consciousness and collective struggle. Creating communism before the Third Disruption is like creating a flying machine before the Second. You could conceive of it – and indeed no less a genius than Leonardo Da Vinci did precisely that – but you could not create it. This was not a failure of will or of intellect, but simply an inevitability of history.

What is more, the means by which the revolution of 1917 was won and defended, through an anti-liberal coup then subject to military invasion by every major power, further limited the possibility for social transformation. Inevitably, this shaped a regime which became supremely hierarchical. Given the odds it faced, both within and beyond its borders, its seven-decade survival remains one of the great political achievements of the last century.

Regardless of history's 'what ifs', FALC is different. Instead it recognises the centrality of human rights, most importantly the right of personal happiness, and seeks to build a society where everyone can access the necessary resources to further that end. This is a politics centred around the recognition, as Franklin Roosevelt once put it, that necessitous people are not free people. In the absence of access to such resources – housing, education, transport, healthcare, information – freedom as self-authorship cannot be said to meaningfully exist. Liberal ends, specifically the individual being uniquely placed to determine their path in life, are impossible without communist means. The possibility of most people finding happiness and meaning is impossible as long as these things are commodities – subject to profit rather than need.

We must understand that appropriate forms of political organisation, just like the utopias we construct, are contingent on the times in which we live. Just as FALC is appropriate for a world where technology leaves us on the cusp of previously unthinkable abundance, the party-form which emerged in response to closed, under-developed societies makes increasingly little sense. The same is true for forms of worker organising, radical or reformist, which are erroneously premised on the society of work enduring forever. That society will not endure, nor should that be our political ambition. The role of the labour movement is to liberate the working class, and therefore all of society, not save a broken system which is passing away.

The vehicles for political transformation change, just like the worlds we reach for. Now we must build a workers' party against work – one whose politics are populist, democratic and open, all while fighting the establishment which, through its power over civil society and the state, won't rest in ensuring FALC never comes to pass.

Electoralism and Society

FALC is only possible now because of the developments of the Third Disruption. The revolution it portends is not simply one that substitutes one ruling class for another, but carries with it a broader shift in ideas, social relations and technologies – what Marx memorably called a mode of production.

What that requires from us, in turn, is to transform this new understanding into a collective subject with specific demands.

In this respect, electoral politics serves a vital purpose. The majority of people are only able to be politically active for brief periods of time. To an extent this is regrettable, the outgrowth of a culture that intentionally cultivates apathy and constrains a wider sense of popular power. Yet it is also a natural response for many who, exhausted by the pace, demands and monotony of work, not to mention family commitments and the sensory overload of the modern world, fail to establish a permanent space for political engagement in their lives. The problem is not, therefore, that most people do not care about politics but rather they cannot afford to care in the face of so many competing demands. While in the last decade, as the status quo has oscillated between inertia and collapse, that has changed slightly, it should not be overstated. At least not yet.

Which is all the more reason why FALC, embedded within a luxury populism, must engage in mainstream, electoral politics. After all, it is often only around elections when large sections of society – particularly the most exploited – are open to new possibilities regarding how society works and able to perceive how previously distinct issues share both common cause and prospective solutions. What is more, the act of voting – even if viewed as devoid of much power in itself – can catalyse a shift to deeper forms of participation and activism. In isolation electoral politics will not give us the world we want, but allied with a constant movement to make the potential of the Third Disruption apparent to everyone – along with the necessity for a collective political response – it shapes the parameters of what is possible.

In addition it must be recognised that the flow of history goes beyond politics, electoral or otherwise. In the shift to FALC we will need new ideas, social relations, forms of daily life and relationships to nature. The political ideologies of the past have often, to their detriment, focused on only one of these at the expense of others: many contemporary anarchists tend to hold social relations as pre-eminent – as if they were distinct from ideas, daily life and work. Leninism, meanwhile, views production, and by extension working-class subjectivity, as critical while ignoring a world whose ideas and technologies are hugely changed from those of the early twentieth century. Elsewhere technological utopians, such as the Californian ideologues of Silicon Valley, view technology as the principal means by which to carve a better future, almost detached from politics, society and history. Finally, certain environmentalists have favoured relations to nature and how we view ourselves in the cosmos, particularly regarding other forms of life, as the primary force that guides their politics. Too often this has come at the expense of a class analysis in understanding exploitation and production under capitalism, and how that system inherently opposes what they want.

Given the stark difference between the world waiting to be built in the shadow of the Third Disruption and the present, the choice is more complex than either choosing to embrace electoralism or renounce state power. Rather we must adopt the disposition of FALC, fitting it to each part of the ensemble that makes history. In each case the driving impetus must always be the same: reaching ahead to the realm of freedom and a world beyond scarcity and jobs; a place where there is the universal freedom to be who we want, and an abundance so plentiful as to seem almost spontaneous. This requires participating in electoral politics and even government, but not being constrained by it.

Against Globalism, towards Internationalism

FALC is internationalist, grasping the integrated nature of the world economy and flows of goods, people, capital and climate systems. It builds on universal values struggled over from Haiti to China for more than two centuries. It accepts that the nation-state, as a tool for the powerful, has concentrated wealth in certain places to the disadvantage of others. To say one country is less developed than another is not to diminish it, but to recognise the global system has intentionally sought to bring such a situation about. The point is not to change the words we use, but the reality they describe.

One of the greatest barriers to such change is the cult of globalism, whose default rhetoric is that the challenges we face are so profound that they can only be resolved through international coordination. On climate change, migration and resource scarcity we repeatedly hear the same refrain: no single nation can solve these problems in isolation. That may well be true but, so far, such talk has served political inertia more than decisive action. Perhaps that was the intention.

The starkest example of this is with climate change: the 1992 Rio Earth Summit was the moment the world began to grasp the devastating consequences of global warming. The resulting conclusion was immediate and would shape globalist presumptions for decades to come: because this challenge was truly planetary in scale only cooperation between states was adequate. Anything less was destined to fall short.

And yet, since then, carbon emissions have significantly increased, with the years immediately following the global financial crisis the worst for emissions in recorded history. The current approach to climate change isn't about 'working together', it's about passivity presented as partnership. The reflex of pointing to the necessity of global solutions –

always conjoined to a form of economic globalisation inter-
changeable with market capitalism – has allowed elites to
evade responsibility. Here 'global coordination' is merely the
international adjunct to capitalist realism, allowing the biggest
polluters – who are also the most powerful nations – to avoid
changing their path.

Which is why we must re-imagine and replicate the prototype politics of the nineteenth century, itself a response to
the Second Disruption as it recast society on a global scale the
first time round. Rather than integration we need imitation,
with the power of the demonstrable example far more com-
pelling than elite interests framed as multilateral compromise.
In response to prototypes the cult of globalism insists they are
ineffective at best and at worst a return to the 1930s – when
nation-states last turned their back on a failing global order.
Such rhetoric is analogous to the anti-utopianism through
which capitalist realism prevails at the domestic level. Nothing
ever changes – and that's the point.

Prototype politics could not be more different, emphasising action and decision, no matter how minor or limited, over
rhetorical cooperation. When we wanted to connect the world
through trains, cable and roads, it was through example and
imitation. When we desired universal literacy and sanitation,
the same applied. When we sought democracy and forms of
government that served the needs of ordinary people, it was
through looking elsewhere and saying, 'Why isn't that us?'
Now the same impulse must apply in creating the institutions,
cultures and technologies to address the problems of our age
– from climate change to ageing and technological unemployment. This requires a basic admission that has been heretical
for much of the left since Fukuyama declared history was
over: quick, effective action can only happen through nation-
states. Complete decarbonisation, in certain respects, is no

greater a challenge than road-building, universal literacy or electrification. It's time for us all to stop waiting and make history once more.

In describing capitalism and what comes after it, Marx wrote incisively about how history contains multiple moving parts:

> In the social production of their existence, men inevitably enter into definite relations, which are independent of their will, namely relations of production appropriate to a given stage in the development of their material forces of production. The totality of these relations of production constitutes the economic structure of society.

He added how these new material relations concurrently created new mental ones too,

> on which arises a legal and political superstructure and to which correspond definite forms of social consciousness. The mode of production of material life conditions the general process of social, political and intellectual life. It is not the consciousness of men that determines their existence, but their social existence that determines their consciousness.

Marx proceeded to say something of supreme importance, especially given what is happening to the price mechanism for information goods, even according to the likes of Paul Romer and Larry Summers:

> At a certain stage of development, the material productive forces of society come into conflict with the existing relations of production or – this merely expresses the same thing in legal terms – with the property relations within the framework of which they have operated hitherto. From forms of development of the productive forces

these relations turn into their fetters. Then begins an era of social
revolution. The changes in the economic foundation lead sooner or
later to the transformation of the whole immense superstructure.

This superstructure, comprising shared popular culture, how
we comprehend nature and even how we author our own
personalities, is in the process of being re-made. A politics
appropriate to FALC understands that and inserts itself into
each terrain, guided always by a simple motto: liberty, luxury
and the pursuit of post-scarcity.

10
Fundamental Principles:
The Break with Neoliberalism

Burn neoliberalism, not people.
Clive Lewis

Carillion's Collapse and the East Coast Line

Although FALC is the political project befitting the Third Disruption, it is a historic moment that will require decades to play out, just as the Second Disruption did following Watt's steam engine. That is no reason to wait, however. Instead we must begin where we stand, by breaking with neoliberalism and building viable alternatives.

So while the political horizon is one of a world beyond work and scarcity, the most pressing task is to discard an orthodoxy built on weak trade unions, precarious labour markets, falling wages and privatisation to break with, in a word, neoliberalism. In each sphere the tide must be turned and, while doing so, placed within an explicit commitment to creating a world entirely different to that of the present.

~

This break must start by switching off the privatisation and outsourcing machine. The reason why is simple: its prevailing logic demands that every public good – from healthcare and education to housing – be sacrificed on the altar of private profit and shareholder value. In this respect privatisation and outsourcing must be viewed as two sides of the same coin. While the former has taken centre stage in undermining the state's provision of public goods – with whole industries privatised en masse over the last fifty years – the latter has proven equally effective in funnelling private profits while maintaining a veneer of public ownership and accountability. The consequences of this have been to make workers poorer and degrade services, often in the name of 'consumer choice', while draining communities of local wealth and know-how.

Shorthand for the failures of outsourcing is the collapse of Carillion, a construction and 'facilities management' company that declared bankruptcy in early 2018. With up to 90 per cent of Carillion's work subcontracted out, as many as 30,000 businesses faced the consequences of its ideologically driven mismanagement. Hedge funds in the City, meanwhile, made hundreds of millions from speculating on its demise.

A favoured pastime of establishment thinkers is to query the very existence of neoliberalism, despite the fact some of the world's most illustrious historians and social scientists have written about it at length. A sufficient response to their line of questioning is simple enough, however, to just utter the name of the former construction giant. How else can you explain the rationale behind a company funded by government contracts that, when it collapses, punishes workers and rewards the casino economy of financial speculation?

Carillion's economic function, particularly after 2010, would have failed to make sense in any other era. With the imposition of austerity, however, it had a vital role to play as it – along with similar companies such as Serco, Sodexo, Capita and G4S – distributed downward pressure on wages while Britain became the world's second-largest outsourcing market.

With the imperative being to push through public sector cuts, particularly in local government, while demonstrating the superiority of the private sector, these companies played a critical role in transferring hundreds of thousands of jobs while paying workers less. Indeed, Britain's private sector employment 'miracle' subsequent to 2010 was possible only because of outsourcing. Its success, however, was inimically tied to falling pay, rising in-work poverty and stagnant productivity.

The breakneck speed of Carillion's downfall shows how outsourcing impoverishes workers in its default setting and, worse still, can cause chaos across whole sectors of the economy. Not only does this jeopardise the delivery of key services and infrastructure but it does so on the back of precarious workers. What is more, multinationals like Carillion effectively use public funds to intensify local poverty while furnishing returns to company shareholders based elsewhere – often in larger, affluent cities. Not only is this model frighteningly effective in its ability to impose falling wages, but also in ensuring capital vacates left-behind towns and cities like never before. As a result, it is responsible for both income and regional inequality.

Yet, while Carillion's collapse demonstrated the pernicious logic of outsourcing, even it failed to match the sheer stupidity of what happened to Britain's East Coast Main Line – connecting the capitals of Edinburgh and London by rail. Returned to public ownership in 2009, when its operator Stagecoach said profit margins were too low in the context of recession, it subsequently became a beacon of excellence, winning twelve industry awards while requiring the lowest level of government investment as a percentage of its total income compared to any private operator. Yes, you read that correctly: the only rail provider in public ownership needed less taxpayer funding than any of the private ones. Unsurprisingly, despite functioning extraordinarily well, the East Coast line was reprivatised in 2013. This was before it had to be 'temporarily' renationalised once more in 2018 when it failed to make a profit, despite subsidies, for its private owners. While the story of the East Coast Main Line is almost funny, the tragedy is that the joke is on us.

Thus, because Britain's private rail providers, just like its outsourcing companies, are nothing more than machines designed to extract value for shareholders at the expense of workers and service users. As well as costing the taxpayer a fortune through subsidies, Britain's rail companies charge some of the most extortionate fares in Europe, with the McNulty report, published in 2011, concluding costs were 40 per cent higher compared to state-owned providers on the Continent.

The reason why the words of certain politicians resonate when they say the system is 'rigged' is because when it comes to the ever-growing swathe of public services subject to privatisation and outsourcing, what they are saying accurately describes everyday reality. Privatisation is not about improving outcomes or services, but pursuing a political agenda which redistributes wealth from the majority of society to a small elite. This is not even the 'free market', but a bizarre hybrid allying the worst features of market capitalism with state socialism.

The Haringey Development Vehicle

While not as economically far-reaching as the collapse of Carillion, or absurd as the East Coast Main Line, the rise and fall of the Haringey Development Vehicle (HDV) in north London offers another example of the neoliberal meat grinder in action.

A joint effort coordinated by the local Labour council and property developer Lendlease, its intention was to respond to the twin problems of the housing crisis and central government reducing local budgets as the result of austerity. In this respect it mirrors outsourcing. There the solution to unemployment is jobs whose wages increase poverty, while the HDV wanted to build homes that ordinary people could not afford. In a London borough where the average home was already fifteen times the median wage, the HDV wasn't a solution to the housing crisis – it entrenched it.

This feedback loop is no accident. Neoliberalism reduces the capacity of public bodies to spend money while simultaneously intensifying social problems like homelessness and poverty. This means the only available options to respond – even if public actors are otherwise minded – are increasingly market-oriented. It is like an ouroboros – the snake of ancient mythology that eats its own tail – intentionally designed to create inequality and a weak incapable state.

That the HDV was overseen by a Labour council was significant. Unlike the East Coast Main Line this was not an obvious example of partisan ideology, where irrationality borders on fanaticism. Instead it was instructive of how neoliberalism can imbricate itself within a fabric of necessity, the refrain of 'there is no alternative' rendered a self-fulfilling prophecy.

The Grenfell Fire

The neoliberal machine has human consequences that go beyond spreadsheets and economic data. Beyond, even, in-work poverty and a life defined by paying ever higher rents to wealthy landlords and fees to company shareholders. As bad as those are they pale beside its clearest historic expression in a generation: the derelict husk of Grenfell Tower – a 24-storey residential block in West London where, in June 2017, seventy-two people lost their lives.

Just days after a general election where Theresa May lost her parliamentary majority, a fire broke which would ravage the building in a manner not seen in Britain for decades. The primary explanation for its rapid, shocking spread across the building – finished in 1974 and intentionally designed to mini-mise the possibility of such an event – was the installation of flammable cladding several years earlier, combined with poor safety standards and no functioning sprinklers – all issues highlighted by the residents' Grenfell Action Group before the fire.

The cladding itself, primarily composed of polyethylene, is as flammable as petroleum. Advances in material science means we should be building homes that are safer, and more efficient, than ever before. Instead a cut-price approach to housing the poor prevails, prioritising external aesthetics for wealthier residents. In the case of Grenfell that meant corners were cut and lives were lost.

This is not a minor political point and shows the very real consequences of 'self-regulation'. It was under the Thatcher government that fire safety standards in homes were deregu-lated, while enforceable requirements were abandoned for 'guidelines' which the building industry could choose to implement or ignore. Months before Grenfell some Tory

MPs had openly spoken of how Brexit meant such a slap-dash approach could be taken further still, with Jacob Rees-Mogg — a prominent right-wing MP — musing how Britain's departure from the EU offered the chance to further reduce environmental and safety standards, 'We could say, if it's good enough in India, it's good enough for here. There's nothing to stop that.'

John McDonnell, Labour's shadow chancellor, caused consternation among the same establishment which takes Rees-Mogg so seriously when he labelled Grenfell 'social murder' claiming that 'political decisions were made which resulted in the deaths of these people'. Yet it was Clive Lewis who incurred the greatest wrath of all when he tweeted an image of the destroyed tower along with the words 'burn neo-liberalism, not people'. That drew gasps of anger from some quarters, but perhaps that was because those eager to defend the status quo grasped that much of the public would agree with the Labour MP.

While not immediately apparent — such is the intention with a political settlement presenting itself as reality — Grenfell was a result of overt political choices. The regulatory changes introduced by Thatcher and extended under New Labour represented a core feature of neoliberal ideology: optimal outcomes are more likely the less you interfere and allow market equilibrium to do its job. That same pernicious ideology had previously provided cover for outsourcing, privatisation and regeneration, despite the facts speaking against it. Now it had led to people dying in their beds.

Despite the magnitude of these issues, a break with all of this is not only plausible but increasingly easy to distinguish. As well as a handbrake on an increasingly dysfunctional present, it is also the first step to FALC. Its primary features are threefold, consisting in the re-localisation of economies through progressive procurement and municipal protectionism; socialising finance and creating a network of local and regional banks and, finally, the introduction of a set of universal basic services (UBS) which take much of the national economy into public ownership. While some of this will resemble the nationalisations of the previous century, much of it will not.

But before changes at a national level can be enacted by governments of the radical left, locally we can start right away. Indeed, in its own way, a revolution from below has already begun.

Ending Neoliberalism 1: The Preston Model

Two centuries ago the inventor Richard Arkwright's home city of Preston was at the leading edge of the Second Disruption as it, like towns and cities across Lancashire, embraced the new technologies of steam-power and coal. More recently, however, Preston had become a backwater, with manufacturing going elsewhere and its early advantage in the Industrial Revolution exhausted long ago. As a result its economic future resembled that of Britain more generally, its best bet being to attract as many low-productivity, service-sector jobs as it could. That explains why, until 2011, local politicians bet the house on a proposed shopping centre, named 'Tithebarn', which they reckoned would create thousands of new jobs.

So when the Tithebarn project finally sank, the city's politicians found themselves out of ideas. The truth was that the global economic crisis which started several years earlier made the development highly unlikely, no matter the wishes of local government. Premised on an economic model of retail and consumer debt, the numbers no longer made sense. Within the broader context of austerity and spending cuts, imposed most harshly on local government, prospects for Preston's economy appeared bleaker than ever.

But then something surprising happened, with Preston turning what seemed like a terminal setback into an opportunity. It did so by taking inspiration from the US city of Cleveland and its own response to similar problems it faced a few years earlier. There the response to a budgetary crisis had been heterodox and unprecedented, with local government refusing the default medicine of privatisation and outsourcing – focusing instead on energising the city's economy through the procurement of 'anchor institutions' like schools, hospitals and universities. In time it proved a success, so much so that the approach came to be titled the 'Cleveland Model'.

Its adoption in Preston, relatively unique in the context of the UK, provided the most unexpected of triumphs. Working with the Manchester-based Centre for Local Economic Strategies (CLES), Preston Council approached the town's anchor institutions in 2011 proposing to redirect as much of their spending as possible back into the local economy. Six agreed to participate. This cooperative effort between civic and public institutions meant that locally focused contracts covered everything from school lunches to large-scale construction projects. All of this meant that while local anchor institutions spent £38 million in Preston in 2013, and £292 million in Lancashire, by 2017 those figures had increased to £111 million and £486 million respectively. While that alone was impressive, even it fails to illustrate the extent of change that locally focused procurement achieved, with a multiplier effect taking off in the city as pounds continually recirculated throughout the local economy. That meant that while real wages for workers in Central Lancashire fell after 2008, much as they did across Britain, in Preston – despite austerity – they actually went up.

Where other authorities privatised, Preston grew its own businesses, even encouraging worker-owned cooperatives. In late 2016 the city was chosen as the best place to live and work in the north-west, ahead of Manchester and Liverpool. Two years later it took the accolade of being Britain's most improved city.

Replicating the Preston Model is the first step in building an economic alternative that breaks with neoliberalism without needing national state power. Despite being delivered in local contexts, the consequences of that would be significant. In the UK, for instance, the NHS alone employs an astonishing 1.4 million people. Between that and the country's schools, colleges, universities and other public institutions, it is clear there is sufficient scale to radically remake the British economy from the bottom up. All in a country which, by international standards, is heavily slanted towards its national capital.

The ambition of scaling the 'Preston Model' goes beyond simple damage limitation or mitigating the worst excesses of austerity. Far from lifeboat socialism, it would be the first step by which regional and national economies are revived. Street by street, town by town, city by city.

How that is achieved is through municipal protectionism, where local, worker-owned business would be actively favoured over multinationals and industry giants. This would not only offer a swift means of reversing privatisation, but simultaneously help build a more resilient, socially just alternative. Whereas the primary values of the present system are cutting costs and maximising shareholder value, here regional and income inequality would be mitigated and a far broader range of ownership models would emerge. In reality this would mean that the only companies able to bid for specific local contracts would have to meet specific criteria, whether it is being based within a certain distance (perhaps ten kilometres or within a county or state); being a worker-owned cooperative; offering organic products or being powered by renewable energy. Shareholder value would be replaced by these kinds of metrics in calculating what makes the most sense.

People's Businesses, People's Banks

Much of this won't be possible without access to credit, with difficulty in accessing finance widely accepted as the single biggest hurdle for cooperatives and worker-owned businesses.

These firms tend to suffer from limited access to long-term finance in capitalist economies, with conventional institutions sceptical of lending to businesses over which they have no control. This lack of support leads to under-investment and a tendency to buckle during moments of financial stress, making cooperative businesses susceptible to acquisition by larger non-worker-owned ones who can access credit more easily. This explains why, despite their 'static' productivity advantages over conventional organisations, over longer periods worker-owned businesses are structurally handicapped – which explains why they presently comprise such a small part of the economy.

Any of the larger national banks – who hold around 80 per cent of deposits in the UK – would prefer to lend £10 million to a single large business than £50,000 to two hundred smaller ones. So if we want to move away from economies based on oligopoly and capital flight, creating a network of local banks and credit unions will be of paramount importance.

Here too a greater focus on the public sector provides part of the solution, with the large pension funds of these same anchor institutions offering more than sufficient capital to start. While Britain's unions rightly resist austerity at the national level, they have around £200 billion of their members' money invested in pensions. By putting this in local development banks, they could not only create more jobs but also ensure better returns for their members. Of course, profit wouldn't be the bottom line, but as John Clancy has written, their returns from investments in overseas equities often prove distinctly underwhelming, which means funds are actively looking for more sustainable and, if necessary, local investments.

In keeping with the new ethos of municipal protectionism, these banks would be similarly restricted in their lending both by amount and geographical area. What is more, their remit would be to maximise social value as well as returns, focusing on energy transition and accelerating specific sectors as well as financing a new wave of worker-owned business.

The positive benefits of growing the cooperative and worker-owned economy are well documented, from helping deal with low productivity to under-investment in small and medium-sized enterprises – not to mention reducing economic and regional inequality. Most importantly, however, within the context of the Third Disruption they offer a practical means by which society can navigate the forward march of automation and, ultimately, artificial intelligence. Despite the immense challenges of both, there is a political solution to a world where labour may well become capital: giving the means of production to workers themselves.

In addition to this network of local banks, central government would create national and regional investment bodies to fund not only businesses but also key infrastructure that delivers social returns – be it reducing emissions or purchasing fixed capital that allows worker-owned enterprises to make more with less. As we'll see in the next chapter this, alongside dramatic changes to the remit of national central banks, will mean a transformed role for finance in the economy.

Return of the State: UBS

As exciting as it is, municipal protectionism and widespread adoption of the 'Preston Model' is not enough in isolation. It may prove the handbrake helping reverse privatisation while providing fertile ground to expand worker-owned business, but it barely scratches the surface when it comes to placing the potential of the Third Disruption in the hands of the people. Which is why Universal Basic Services (UBS) must be offered alongside it.

The classic way of expressing this idea is nationalisation, with government owning and controlling a range of industries and services. Such a model is familiar to many. After the Second World War the modern welfare state, across Europe in particular, was a central player in much of the economy – from energy and education to the commanding heights of manufacture and mining. Elsewhere other countries experimenting with forms of state socialism, often under the political influence of the USSR, dispensed with market production altogether, privileging what they called economic rights – particularly for work – over civil and political ones. Even in the mixed-market economies, however, there were aspects of this second approach, with perhaps the most obvious being Britain's National Health Service. Created in 1948, and still free at the point of use, it remains the largest publicly funded healthcare system anywhere in the world.

While its critics like to paint the NHS as outdated and old-fashioned, unable to keep pace with the demands of a rapidly changing world, it's the opposite which is true. Despite underfunding, it is consistently rated among the best healthcare systems of the wealthy nations, proving particularly outstanding when it comes to efficiency. Whereas the United States spends around 17 per cent of its GDP on healthcare

– approximately \$9,892 per person – Britain spends just \$4,192. And yet it is Britain which provides universal coverage and enjoys better outcomes on a range of key measures, from infant mortality to deaths in childbirth and life expectancy.

As the five crises unfold – from societal ageing to climate change and technological unemployment – it won't be a case of no longer being able to afford systems like the NHS, as many of today's politicians are all-too-eager to say. Rather it will necessitate a rejection of less-efficient models which aren't universal or free at the point of use. As well as being the most ethical way of distributing the abundance made possible by the Third Disruption, the five crises also require universalism from the perspective of efficiency.

Far from an idea of marginal interest, UBS has become increasingly central in contemporary conversations about the provision of public services. This is most apparent in a 2016 report titled 'Social Prosperity for the Future', published by the Institute for Global Prosperity at University College London. While the report did not explicitly establish its proposals within the context of the Third Disruption, it did situate them within a set of challenges comparable to those of the five crises, identifying six public goods – besides healthcare – which should be reconstituted to more closely resemble the NHS and Britain's healthcare model. These are education, democracy and legal services, shelter, food, transport and information.

The IGP report was eager to emphasise that UBS isn't solely a response to crises whose emergence is relatively recent, but also the means by which citizens can enjoy fuller lives, accessing the resources necessary to be who they want. Thus the broader hope is to mitigate 'unfreedom' – the dependence on economic forces beyond our control which, for nearly all of us, determine how life turns out.

Not all seven services outlined in the UCL report are necessary in the transition to FALC – at least not initially. Indeed,
alongside municipal protectionism and a worker-led economy,
it is taken here that only five need be established: housing,
transport, education, healthcare and information. As UBS, the
intention for each is to become free public goods accessible to
everyone – not as commodities for exchange and profit, but
as the foundational resources on which to build their lives.
That is not to say private ownership of housing, for instance,
would be prohibited – it would not, but there would be a
guarantee that the state would meet an individual's housing
needs if required. Market production and the price mechanism
would endure, but this would become progressively rarer in
those areas classified as universal basic services. With energy,
labour, and resources wanting, like information, to be free,
history and extreme supply would be on the side of UBS.

As a consequence, UBS will diffuse incrementally. In transport
it might resemble the UK's 'Freedom Pass' – which allows
free travel on local bus services for those over sixty – being
extended to everyone. This is sensible – as we've already seen,
transport sits at the intersection of post-scarcity in energy and
labour with extreme supply from renewable power (energy)
and autonomous driving (labour) meaning the cost of public
transport will fall precipitously. This should be to the benefit
of users, citizens and workers – not profiteers. The UBS of
progressively expanding free public transportation is the best
way of ensuring precisely that.

Similarly, in healthcare, the rise of ultra-low-cost technologies in the areas of gene sequencing, therapies and editing
will mean that a few decades from now public healthcare
will be cheaper to administer with each passing year. But this
will only be of collective benefit if we reject the notion that

edited genes are the same as pharmaceutical drugs and must be subject to patent and the profit motive. Instead, the gains of healthcare becoming a true information technology should be socialised as we eliminate genetically inherited conditions like Parkinson's, Huntington's and sickle cell disease – much like we did with smallpox in the twentieth century.

Even such breakthroughs, tremendous and unprecedented as they would be, would represent just the first step, as the arrival of virtually free gene sequencing – which would allow us to all but eliminate early-years mortality and locate cancers at 'Stage 0' – moves medicine from responsive to preventative. Again, rather than propping up the profits of private business while putting millions of healthcare workers out of a job, that should mean free, universal healthcare for everyone. The alternative of allowing market rationing amid conditions of such abundance, and for matters of literal life and death, is barbaric.

The same trends are evident in housing, education and information – understood here as media production and internet connectivity. Just a few decades from now paying for a bus, or an internet connection, or a university degree or renting a home, need not be an issue. In each instance payment might feel as counter-intuitive as it would today if you were invoiced for starting an email account or checking the accuracy of a date on Wikipedia. And why shouldn't it? After all, resources, energy, health, labour and food – just like information – want to be free. It is this fundamental tendency which underwrites why a constantly expanding provision of UBS, in line with extreme supply, should be a central demand for twenty-first-century politics.

Alongside a shift to municipal protectionism, the implementation of UBS would create a much larger role for the state

– although given extreme supply, perhaps not as much as one might think. The state will be crucial in procurement with local worker cooperatives building homes, hospitals and schools as well as performing catering, maintenance, cleaning and support services. Under the neoliberal model these are the ground zero of the outsourcing economy, with workers subject to constant attacks over wages and working standards while users endure ever-poorer outcomes. In the transition to FALC, however, and with UBS adopting a central position in the economy, the leverage of anchor institutions will only expand. While automation will eliminate as much work as possible, those jobs which remain – most likely because of Moravec's Paradox – will increasingly be performed by worker-owned businesses, completely transforming how we relate to society, work and one another.

Importantly, UBS should be presented as an expanded set of rights, an upgrade on the constitutions that emerged alongside the Second Disruption in places such as Corsica, the United States, France and Haiti. Legal and political rights will remain of critical importance, but it will be increasingly acknowledged that these mean little without access to economic and social resources. Finally, we will have realised that liberal ends of personal fulfilment and self-authorship mean little without socialist means. The technology of the Third Disruption, combined with the politics of FALC, bring them finally within reach.

Decarbonisation

While societal ageing may be the larger problem over the next half a century, climate change is without doubt the greatest challenge confronting humanity. Although its scale is so significant precisely *because* it will unfold in a multigenerational

– and therefore unpredictable – manner, it must be present generations that take decisive action.

Yet more than simply an intervention determining the future capacity of our planet to maintain life, the politics of energy transition must also articulate its ambition of bringing limitless energy to the world's rich and poor alike. That is the prize on offer with solar and wind, almost as much as saving the planet, and should be stated as such when demanding energy transition alongside UBS. Switching to renewable energy won't just mitigate increasingly chaotic climate systems, it will also deliver greater prosperity for all of us.

But while the opportunities are huge, and the political scope for integrating ecology and economic development increasingly clear, there is little time to act. The reality is we have to decarbonise the world economy by the middle of this century to stand any chance of halting warming beyond two degrees centigrade.

The demand, therefore, is as audacious as it is simple. The Global North must reduce its carbon dioxide emissions by an annual rate of 8 per cent each year for the decade following 2020. Then, starting in 2030, the Global South will embark on the same journey at precisely the same rate. If successful that will mean a full, global transition to renewable energy by 2040. Of course, that is easier said than done, and a complete transition to renewable energy in little more than two decades would be the greatest feat of collective action in human history. But the truth is we have no alternative. Fortunately, the technology we already possess means it is entirely possible. What has been missing, until now, is political will.

Indeed, we don't need to invent new means of generating and storing renewable energy. Rather we must accelerate the progress of already-available technologies. Even on present trends, as detailed in Chapter Five, fossil fuels will become increasingly obsolete over the coming decades. The challenge, then, is to hasten this shift while ensuring the Global South isn't left behind in a manner reminiscent of industrialisation in the early nineteenth century. A heightened emphasis on developing nations will serve to speed decarbonisation, especially given all new demand between now and 2035 will come from the Global South. Furthermore, the transition to renewables isn't just about advancing green technologies, which are on their way regardless (though not quickly enough), but making sure they are in the hands of the people. Because of its modular and distributed nature, this revolution should be about the democratisation of energy as much as its sustainability.

As with scaling up worker-owned business and cooperatives at the municipal level, the mechanism by which this will be advanced is socially controlled finance. In the Global North, where mass decarbonisation will start, this will be far simpler to administer as many countries have already hit a ceiling in terms of population and per capita energy use. What is more, they tend to enjoy robust state institutions and a significant base of renewable energy capacity.

The worker-led economy will be financed by locally based and geographically restricted institutions. But because of the shortened timeframe, financing energy transition will be the responsibility for much larger National Energy Investment Banks (NEIBs) operating through regional hubs and capitalised – depending on the country – to the tune of hundreds of billions of pounds.

Alongside financing renewable energy generation and storage for public buildings, homes and workplaces, with this new infrastructure being democratically owned at the local level, these banks will also offer credit for local energy cooperatives. Such measures will be accompanied by the financing of energy efficiency programmes whose intention will be to make conventional heating systems unnecessary and smart systems and LED lighting ubiquitous. We have known how to minimise energy consumption for heating – the primary issue in the colder countries of Europe, Russia and North America – for decades, the problem being market-based solutions have failed to materialise. With that in mind, the rate of change could easily exceed the 8 per cent annual target for colder countries – especially when one considers they could likely halve energy consumption simply through intelligent heat conservation.

By 2030 the world's wealthier countries would see their CO_2 emissions fall to virtually zero, their poorer citizens no longer subject to the scourge of energy poverty and 'excess deaths' in winter. What is more, that would just be the start, because the technologies that make all of this possible will – unlike fossil fuels – keep on getting cheaper.

For the Global South the solution will be more complex. Whereas the task in the wealthier countries is to accelerate a set of already-observable tendencies for lower GDP countries substantial changes to actually existing globalisation will be pivotal. That means the task is somewhat harder here, as it necessitates a coordinated multilateral response. But as already outlined, the rewards of energy abundance are greatest of all for the Global South. More than simply 'catching up', many of these countries – by virtue of geographical good fortune – enjoy the highest solar potential on Earth. While the transition from fossil fuels will ultimately mean energy gets permanently cheaper for everyone irrespective of where they live, of almost equal importance is how historically underdeveloped countries will enjoy a comparative advantage.

Take Saudi Arabia. While it is an affluent country as a result of its oil wealth, as with other countries across the Middle East, much of Africa and south Asia, it has huge solar potential. While it might be unsurprising that the Kingdom is increasingly involved in solar technology, the scale of a deal it negotiated in early 2018 – to build 200 terawatts of solar capacity across the country by 2030 – came as a shock. For context, that is four times the peak use for the whole of the United Kingdom, a country with a population more than twice its size. While Saudi Arabia has the funds to build such historically unprecedented infrastructure – when completed it will be the greatest solar development in history – this is precisely the scale and ambition that is needed to move the world beyond fossil fuels by 2040.

But given that most of the Global South lacks those kinds of resources, any reliance on petrodollars to fund transition is inadequate. Just like the wealthier countries, that will mean National Energy Investment Banks coupled with significant reforms to the World Bank – an organisation which is, at present, primarily responsible for providing loans to poorer countries for capital programmes. Currently comprised of two institutions – the International Bank for Reconstruction and Development (IBRD) and the International Development Association (IDA) – its stated goal is the reduction of global poverty through the promotion of foreign investment and international trade. But while its intended purpose is laudable, there can be little doubt it is failing. That is because its understanding of development is built on an ideological commitment to free trade and a worldview which, in the context of the Third Disruption, makes increasingly little sense.

As our technologies move to extreme supply, such fidelity to market fundamentalism will only serve to entrench poverty rather than eliminate it. Without recognising this problem, global capitalism will under-develop these regions more acutely than ever, meaning that what should be the energy powerhouses of tomorrow will remain unable to even guarantee access to electricity for their citizens.

Which is why, given the demands of transitioning from fossil fuels in the Global South – coupled with what successful transition might mean for economic development and climate change – a third body should be added to the World Bank Group. This would be called the International Bank for Energy Prosperity, its mission being to help create NEIBs in poorer countries which would be funded by a new 'One Planet Tax'. The purpose of this tax, global in its extent, would be simple: to channel resources from affluent countries – who are overwhelmingly responsible for climate change – to poorer ones, who are set to disproportionately suffer its most adverse consequences.

The revenues for this tax would be raised by imposing a $25 fee on every tonne of CO_2 emitted in high-GDP countries. As well as helping fund energy transition in the Global South this would also create an additional incentive among the wealthier nations to decarbonise in the decade following 2020, not to mention stimulating a market in carbon sequestration technologies. A reasonable projection is that this alone would raise around $250 billion a year – not an insignificant sum. If the measure fell short in raising as much, which would represent success from the perspective of decarbonisation, the remainder would be generated from countries paying into the fund based on a GDP per capita basis.

In addition to capitalising EIBs in some of the poorest countries in the world, whose role would be precisely the same as their equivalents in the Global North, the One Planet Tax would also pay for technology transfer and research and development into modular renewable solutions adapted to low-infrastructure, low-income environments. Here the aim would be to create an energy analogue to the mobile phone of the early twenty-first century. The diffusion of abundant energy in low-income countries will look nothing like the national infrastructures of the last century. If household PV does spread as quickly as mobile phones have since the 2000s, seemingly unbridgeable gulfs between the world's rich and poor in electricity, clean drinking water and living standards will be overcome in an extraordinarily short span of time. This would be an energy revolution – with Asian and African characteristics.

In the event of complete decarbonisation by 2040, as sovereign states not only fund the diffusion but democratic ownership of green energy infrastructure, then the achievement will extend beyond averting runaway climate change – as magnificent as that will be. It would also mean those historically poorer countries along the equator would possess some of the most abundant, cheapest energy on Earth. This, alongside the delivery of UBS, would underpin similar leaps forward in health, education and housing, enabling meaningful development like never before and helping sever the chains of economic dependence that have characterised centuries of plunder and exploitation. Amid recent calls for reparations to atone for the historic injustices of the Atlantic slave trade and European empires, a One World Tax would turn a timely idea into a concrete demand. Wealthier countries must pay for the clean energy of poorer ones.

11
Reforging the Capitalist State

It measures everything, in short, except that which makes life worthwhile.

Robert Kennedy

Money for Nothing

While the state guaranteeing the provision of certain goods has a long history, particularly in the twentieth century, it is the idea of a Universal Basic Income – the 'UBI' – which seems to have attracted greater curiosity in recent years. The reason why isn't difficult to understand. Many are convinced of its ability to address multiple aspects of the five crises, with it being uniquely capable of responding to 'the conjunction of growing inequality, a new wave of automation, and a more acute awareness of the ecological limits to growth'.

The impulse behind UBI is as simple as Universal Basic Services, except rather than certain goods being free at the point of use for everybody, every citizen is given a fixed amount of money at regular intervals. It is, simply understood, a wage without work.

For those eager to proclaim the radical, disruptive potential of UBI, this severing of payment from work presents a challenge to capitalism itself, undermining its vital disciplinary function over workers who have to sell their labour in order to live. At a minimum, its advocates claim, this would serve to strengthen labour in relation to capital – much as trade unions did in the nineteenth and twentieth centuries – offering an immediate social democratic solution within the context of automation and technological unemployment.

This may all prove to be the case. The truth is we don't really know because UBI has never before been tested at sufficient scale before. What we can be certain of, however, is that its consequences would depend on the broader political environment in which it is introduced. Under a progressive or socialist government, UBI might well prove to be a potent measure empowering ordinary people and giving them the ability to demand higher pay. Alternatively, it may just as easily be the means by which to complete the full marketisation of the welfare state, a capitulation to neoliberalism rather than an alternative to it. It is its range of possibilities, from potentially liberatory to Thatcherism on steroids, which explains why two of the most important thinkers in the history of neoliberalism, Milton Friedman and F.A. Hayek, can be counted among its enthusiasts.

A more immediate criticism of UBI, however, and one that is easier to anticipate in detail, is that it would cost a huge amount while not achieving particularly much. In 2016 the British think tank Compass modelled a UBI that paid £284 ($380) a month to every working-age adult and smaller payments for others. This would stand alongside, rather than replace, extant social programmes adding £170 billion a year to public spending – equivalent to 6.5 per cent of the country's GDP and more than is presently given to the NHS.

Yet despite such massive investment, the projected returns prove distinctly underwhelming. Compass predicted that even with this extraordinary intervention, child poverty would only fall from 16 to 9 per cent, while pensioner poverty would stay broadly the same at 14 per cent. As Luke Martinelli put it, 'An affordable UBI is inadequate, and an adequate UBI is unaffordable.' Given the sums involved, far more progressive measures should be pursued instead.

Which is why a programme of UBS is preferable, with the universal right to particular resources such as housing and healthcare being more politically robust than a wage, and easily integrated within a luxury populism. UBS also makes more intuitive sense to the public at large, being reminiscent of national ownership – whose return is increasingly popular. Compare that to UBI, a policy whose consequences are uncertain to all involved save for the fact it would be, by far, the single greatest government expenditure.

Furthermore, preferring UBS to UBI makes a great deal of sense within the context of the Third Disruption and the turn to extreme supply. As the price for everything shifts ever closer to zero, this will imperil production for exchange and profit, meaning the price mechanism is an increasingly inefficient way of allocating resources. What is more UBS begins the work of communism in the present, articulating resources necessary to a decent life – from housing to healthcare – as human rights rather than potential sources of profit. Necessitous people are not free people, and the UBS decisively ends such necessity.

Central Banks as Central Planners

A fundamental deceit lies at the heart of modern market systems. We are told that the old Soviet economy was centrally planned, with the infamous Gosplan agency at the heart of the USSR's economic life. Modern capitalist economies, by contrast, are 'free', with autonomous actors participating in market exchange to maximise their own interests and, fortunately, promoting the general welfare too.

Only this isn't true. Central planning is a significant feature in 'free market' economies, from Walmart to Amazon. The primary site for this is central banks, however, whose decisions – despite claims to being impartially technocratic – are based on political priorities for inflation, employment and asset prices. Private banks perform something similar on a smaller scale, deciding what projects are to receive a share of society's resources and enforce the 'judgement of the market' on those which lose money.

The claim of central bank 'independence', a favoured policy at the apogee of capitalist realism during the 2000s, is as absurd a conjecture as the end of history itself. Here the pivotal actors within modern capitalist economies, who make specific choices that privilege certain groups at the cost of others, think of themselves as neutral with 'common sense' prevailing rather than ideology.

Beyond highlighting the fact that the decisions of central banks are themselves deeply political, the goal for those pursuing FALC should be to openly champion political banking. Rather than joining the cries of 'end the Fed', a phrase heard with increasing regularity on the libertarian right, the response should be the opposite: to demand that the intentional, conscious planning at the heart of modern capitalism be repurposed to socially useful ends rather than socially destructive ones. That the Bank of England and US Federal Reserve share numerous characteristics with the Soviet Gosplan should be the basis for political hopes rather than lamented as obstructing the mythical operation of a 'truly' free market. Such a thing has never existed, nor can it.

So what is to be done with the central banks of the early twenty-first century? As with the introduction of municipal protectionism, UBS and the shift to a post-carbon energy infrastructure, change will be both decisive and incremental. What must happen immediately, however, is an end to the monetarist policies which have privileged low inflation at the cost of all else. This central pillar of neoliberalism – sold as part of a broader set of policies during the Thatcher and Reagan years – was identified as necessary in dealing with issues of inflation which increasingly beset the economies of the Global North after the early 1970s. After that, the ideologues said, sustainable economic growth was only possible with low, controlled inflation, and central banks had to play a leading role in the new orthodoxy. Yet, as already discussed, average GDP growth has fallen in each decade since. It has become increasingly hard to argue that the purpose of low inflation is anything other than to advantage asset-holders and creditors over those with debts. In short, monetarism and low-inflation ideology is just one part of the rigged system that serves speculative capital and the wealthy at the expense of everything else.

Which is why in the transition to FALC the role of central banks will change once more, the emphasis moving away from low inflation – at present the Bank of England has a target of 2 per cent – to rising wages, high productivity and affordable house prices. This would be part of a broader programme to politicise central banks as central planners and democratise these supposedly 'neutral' institutions.

In terms of how central banks might keep a lid on property prices – presently a major source of value and profit in financialised economies – a paper released by the IPPR think tank in July 2018 is instructive. It argues that the necessary measures are relatively straightforward, with the Bank's Financial Policy Committee best placed to set a target for house price inflation – similar to how the Monetary Policy Committee is presently tasked with consumer price inflation. Under such a target the Bank of England would aim to keep nominal house price inflation at zero while the UBS of housing was guaranteed through a programme of mass home building by central and local government. The report outlines how that target would be met by using macro-prudential tools such as capital requirements, loan-to-value, and debt-to-income ratios while restricting overseas purchases of UK residential property. This, alongside building millions of new homes, would almost certainly mean house prices would fall over the space of a generation.

In regard to productivity, similar targets would be given to central banks – something recently advocated by the British Labour Party. This would incentivise funding the productive rather than speculative economy while increasing wages alongside the ratio of fixed capital to variable. Automation that serves the needs of people should be the heart of monetary as well as fiscal policy.

Repressing the Speculative Economy

As well as financing the economy of tomorrow – whether it be at the national level with central banks as they turn to meaningful metrics other than inflation, or local and regional banks funding worker-owned business – a critical task remains in shrinking the size and power of the speculative financial economy. In many countries, particularly Britain and the United States, capping house prices would be a major step toward achieving that. And moving the emphasis away from inflation-busting would mean creditors no longer enjoy the structural bias they presently do.

But it is also clear that additional protocols will be needed in the management of capital flows. A financial transactions tax on currency trading would be an obvious means of capital control. This tax would be levied at two variable rates: the lower one, which could be as little as 0.005 per cent would be imposed on day-to-day transactions in order to curb volatility, while a higher one would be deployed in the case of speculative attacks or large capital outflows – a probability as ever more countries turn their back on neoliberalism. The necessary conditions for implementing the higher rate, which would be akin to a 'windfall tax' on profits made from speculative attacks, would again be determined by central banks. Yet regardless of that it would be a crucial instrument against global financial interests whose primary weapon is capital mobility across borders.

But that isn't everything, because the final piece in changing the financial architecture to enable the transition to FALC is perhaps the most important. It involves the progressive socialisation of finance and capital markets.

A Socialised Capital Market

As the end drew nearer for the USSR and Eastern Bloc in the late 1980s, dissident intellectuals were eager to draw lessons from a system which despite its best intentions was now failing to deliver rising living standards on a par with the West. Włodzimierz Brus and Kazimierz Łaski were two such thinkers, socialist economists and followers of the distinguished Marxist–Keynesian Michał Kalecki. In *From Marx to the Market*, published in England in 1989, they assessed the prospects for socialist economics with the demise of the Soviet project. Both had been influential proponents of democratic reforms for decades, with Łaski forced to leave Poland in 1968 and Brus in 1972.

Marx to Market offered an extended revision of an argument offered by Brus in 1961 in *The General Problems of the Functioning of the Socialist Economy*. There, heavily influenced by the thinking of Kalecki, he argued that both democracy and market mechanisms were necessary in the transition to socialism.

This was expanded further in 1989 with Brus and Łaski claiming that under market socialism, publicly owned firms would have to be autonomous – much as they are in market capitalist systems – and that this would necessitate a socialised capital market. In the countries of actually existing socialism, even in 1989, this was as heretical as it had been in the early 1960s, with such thinking at odds with the top–down, nationally controlled industries that came to dominate the economic landscape not only of the USSR but other countries such as Cuba and North Korea.

Rather than industrial national monoliths being lauded as the archetype of economic efficiency, the authors argued for a completely different kind of socialism declaring, 'The role of the owner-state should be separated from the state as an authority in charge of administration ... (enterprises) have to become separated not only from the state in its wider role but also from one another.' For their critics this was worryingly reminiscent of capitalism and production for profit.

Yet this is effectively what the cooperatives and worker-owned businesses, bootstrapped under the municipal protectionism outlined in the previous chapter, would look like. With the introduction of UBS and a historic intervention in decarbonising the economy, these kinds of enterprise could rapidly become the backbone of economies across the Global North and South. But worker ownership will need socialised finance, with credit explicitly favouring businesses and cooperatives whose objectives extend beyond just profit. As a result, national investment banks – alongside municipal banks and NEIBs – will need to be founded, their role being to specifically amplify extreme supply, underpin UBS and ameliorate the five crises.

The End of GDP

Peter Drucker may have been the leading theorist of information in the modern economy, but he did so as a management theorist rather than economist or historian. It was this obsession with management which inspired his most memorable quote 'if you can't measure it, you can't manage it' – a favourite dictum of executives for decades and now the calling card of data-driven performance.

It is true in public policy as much as anywhere else. While it is critical to outline the policies necessary to break with neoliberalism and begin the shift to FALC, this means little if new metrics of success aren't also created. If we continue to measure things which mean little in dealing with the five crises – while failing to capture the essence of value as information becomes progressively more important – then whatever merits central bank reform or UBS might have, the pursuit of FALC will fall short. Simply put, we need new ways of measuring success appropriate for the Third Disruption, rather than the Second. Ultimately that means leaving the world of GDP, or gross domestic product, behind us.

Today GDP is the principal measure of economic activity. When GDP is rising, the economy can be said to be growing; when it is in reverse, this marks a recession. The information it expresses is the value of all economic transactions within a fixed period of time, usually a year. That is, all the goods and services that are produced, sold and purchased.

Given its centrality in any discussion of what kind of economic model is preferable, it's easy to presume that the idea of GDP is as old as capitalism itself – that it was perhaps contrived by the likes of Adam Smith or David Ricardo. Yet to the contrary, it is a relatively recent development, devised by the economist Simon Kuznets in the 1930s in response to the Great Depression. It turns out that the central imperative of modern societies – that economic growth should be pursued as an end in itself – only started to reign supreme a century and a half after the Second Disruption began.

Perhaps even more surprising is that scepticism of it is almost as old as the measure itself. In 1968 Robert Kennedy spoke of how GDP 'measures everything, in short, except that which makes life worthwhile'. While Kuznets himself cautioned that 'the welfare of a nation can scarcely be inferred from a measure of national income'. Even for its inventor, GDP was always limited in understanding the broader determinants of a truly successful society.

But besides those older judgements regarding the often zealous manner in which GDP was used, by the late 1980s another criticism began to emerge. Now, some said, it was no longer capable of even measuring economic growth properly. This was most famously expressed by the economist Robert Solow when he claimed in 1987 that 'you can see the computer age everywhere but the productivity statistics.' That conclusion was a response to the 'productivity paradox' which so troubled economists at the time – namely, how investment in information technology over the 1980s had a seemingly negligible impact on productivity measures, which actually slowed over the decade.

But what if, rather than digital technologies failing to increase productivity, the changes they wrought were so significant as to require a new way of measuring success altogether? What if we are only at the beginning of an economic shift so profound that, as the Third Disruption continues to unfold, GDP will prove increasingly incapable of capturing all the value being created?

I would submit that this is now happening. Extreme supply is causing deflation across many sectors, and the Third Disruption is evaporating whole swathes of GDP. As the marginal cost of producing goods and services moves closer to zero in more and more sectors, the result is more free, non-market transactions will take place. Even where the market can respond and keep certain goods within the price mechanism – as proven with Spotify's rental model as a response to digital file-sharing – extreme supply still means reduced net circulation. Today few would pay £15 for a music album, something that two decades ago everyone in the Global North took for granted. That explains why twenty years after the digitisation of the music industry began, the value of the market remains substantially smaller, even despite the increasing popularity of streaming services such as Spotify and Tidal. In 1999 the music industry generated revenues worth some $14.6 billion in the United States, a figure which had fallen to $7.65 billion by 2016 – and that's not accounting for inflation.

In terms of how we conventionally understand GDP, those figures should signify disaster – reflecting how fewer people are listening to their favourite musicians than before. Except the opposite is true. Extreme supply in information goods – of which music is a paradigmatic example – means more people are listening to more music than ever, it's just failing to show up in the numbers we think matter most.

Another example that goes beyond established assumptions in market economics is Wikipedia. Free at the point of consumption and co-produced almost entirely by a team of volunteers, it is superior to any other encyclopaedia ever created. Indeed, the success of Wikipedia meant that in 2012, after being in print for 244 years, its famed rival, the *Encyclopaedia Britannica*, went completely online. While its print editions previously sold for $1,400 the new internet-based service cost just $17 a month – and yet still it couldn't hope to compete. While some deride the importance of Wikipedia as a resource, ask yourself how much you've used it and, subsequently, how much value you would place on it. I'll guarantee it's far more than zero. The fact 99 per cent of its articles rank in the top ten results for any Google search speaks for itself.

These two trends – of deflationary prices in the market economy and production of more free things in its non-market equivalent – will ultimately render GDP irrelevant as a means to measure people's quality of life, especially once the post-capitalist state accelerates such tendencies. That, alongside the implementation of UBS, means GDP will only deteriorate as a significant measure of anything, as limited as it already was. What is more it will fail to calculate those things that matter most in the context of the five crises, including atmospheric CO_2, the health and lifespan of the elderly, environmental degradation, access to clean air and drinking water, mental wellbeing and work that is socially and emotionally satisfying.

Which is why the post-capitalist state would move towards an 'Abundance index' accounting for all of this, while integrating the emerging economic model of ever fewer things paid for with money. Initially such an index would integrate CO_2 emissions, energy efficiency, the falling cost of energy, resources and labour, the extent to which UBS had been delivered, leisure time (time not in paid employment), health and lifespan, and self-reported happiness. Such a composite measure, no doubt adapted to a variety of regional and cultural differences, would be how we assess the performance of post-capitalist economies in the passage to FALC. This would be a scorecard for social progress assessing how successful the Third Disruption is in serving the common good.

Just as it took generations for the Second Disruption to find its measure of progress with GDP, the Third Disruption is facing a similar challenge. What we know for certain is that an already emerging model – with less monetary exchange and a shift to rents – creates too much abundance to be accurately measured by currently available means. This will only intensify further over time.

Universal basic services will be fundamental in the transition to FALC and will be progressively easier to provide. But the measure of success can't be the volume of transactions through the price system – to do so would be using the definition of progress that belongs to a world already passing away.

12

FALC: A New Beginning

Socialism is not evolution's last and perfect product or the end of history,
but in a sense only the beginning.

Isaac Deutscher

The relationship between technology and politics is a com-
plicated one. Melvin Kranzberg put it best in his 'Six Laws
of Technology' when he outlined the first of those laws:
'Technology is neither good nor bad; nor is it neutral.' In other
words, how technology is created and used, and to whose
advantage, depends on the political, ethical and social contexts from which it emerges. To paraphrase Marx, technology
makes history – but not under conditions of its own making.

Perhaps that's what Kranzberg meant with his sixth law,
'All history is relevant, but the history of technology is the
most relevant.' Technology may not determine history, but it
can disrupt and shape it like nothing else. The technological
shift of the First Disruption embodies that law. Cities, culture
and writing – themselves the basis for ever more complex
forms of social organisation – were shaped by agriculture,

the domestication of animals and crops, and a practical understanding of heredity.

That is not to say technology determines all paths. Indeed,
there is a case to be made that the technologies of the Second
Disruption – principally Watt's steam engine – were merely
the final element in the broader transition to capitalism. Here
industrial innovation came after centralised states, the emergence of a class of 'landless labourers' and certain ideas of
private and intellectual property. So, while technologies can
herald new moments in history, they are just as likely to
depend on what went before.

The Third Disruption appears to express both tendencies.
Rather than technologies like AI, renewable energy and gene
editing being exogenous disruptors of the status quo, they
have developed alongside new ideas of nature, selfhood and
forms of production.

Take the green movement as just one example. In any
successful transition to meat without animals – as outlined
in Chapter Eight – its worldview, advanced over decades
of activism, will have played a decisive role. While technologically speaking synthetic meat is impossible without
digitisation, these products were only created in response
to vegan and vegetarian demand, as well as their developers
having concerns about the impact of agriculture on climate
change and animal welfare.

The same is true for renewable energy. Here too the
green movement has been a vital player in making the issue
of climate change salient to the wider public. While political
failure at the international level is undeniable, with nation-
states failing to sufficiently reduce CO_2 emissions over the last
twenty-five years, that does not mean the movement's legacy
is one of defeat. The increased capacity of wind and solar
to meet our energy needs again results from technological

innovation which would not have materialised without generations of campaigners demanding a shift away from fossil fuels. Fracking bans in a constantly growing number of countries, municipalities and cities, are only the latest testament to that.

Elsewhere the impulse to automation and the application of the experience curve are an outgrowth of competition, the prevailing logic of capitalism. This has presaged the incessant replacement of labour with fixed capital while seeing declining costs of production for just about everything. While levels of automation have arguably slowed over recent decades, primarily as a result of wages being pushed so low that replacing workers wasn't profitable, the context within which waves of automation will unfold in coming decades matters. Contradictions internal to capitalism make a crisis of technological unemployment, terminal under-consumption and rising inequality unavoidable.

So technology is of critical importance, but so are the ideas, social relations and politics which accompany it. Thus in making sense of how we arrived at the present, from AI to synthetic meat, we must look at social movements – from Indigenous land rights to protecting animal welfare – as much as the underlying dynamics of extreme supply.

But more than allowing us to comprehend an increasingly complex present, placing the relationship between technology and history within a broader constellation of actors allows us to chart the course for a better future. It helps us understand why some things transpire at certain moments rather than others and why, until now, communism was impossible.

Futures Deferred

Some visionaries have such powers of foresight that their ideas aren't consonant with the times in which they live. John

Wycliffe, a fourteenth-century priest who oversaw a translation of the Latin Bible into English, was one such person. The heterodox Wycliffe opposed core tenets of the church including veneration of saints, monasticism and even the papacy. Yet Wycliffe, whose Bible was spread across England a century before Martin Luther was born, remains a peripheral figure in the history of the Reformation.

The reason why is technology. While Wycliffe's Bible was widely distributed, it was not a printed document in the modern sense – meaning it could never find as large an audience as the vernacular pamphlets and books of a century later. That Martin Luther came to be the seminal figure in the Reformation was, therefore, a consequence of technological innovation rather than personal charisma or new ideas. By the early 1500s, 200 million printed books were in circulation across Europe – a revolution in information even more seismic than the arrival of the internet.

Yet to claim that technology, in particular the printing press, caused the Reformation is absurd – especially when its central ideas had a genealogy which could be traced back for centuries. Where it did prove decisive, however, was in making certain events unfold which had seemed previously impossible – even by the protagonists themselves. When he pinned his '95 Theses' to the church door in Wittenberg on 31 October 1517, Luther had no idea what would happen next.

Within six weeks printed editions appeared simultaneously in Leipzig, Nuremberg and Basel. Not long after came German translations – the initial document was in Latin – with these capable of being read by a much wider audience. Friedrich Myconius, a friend of Luther, would later write, 'hardly 14 days had passed when these propositions were known throughout Germany and within four weeks almost all of Christendom was familiar with them.'

Luther's first pamphlet to be written in German, the 'Sermon on Indulgences and Grace', would be reprinted fourteen times in 1518 alone. Of the 6,000 pamphlets published in German between 1520 and 1526, some 1,700 were to be editions of Luther's works. In all, that meant around 2 million pamphlets of his work were published in the decade after he pinned his original theses – hand-written and in Latin – to the door at Wittenberg. In short, technology made what was impossible in Wycliffe's time seemingly inevitable in Luther's.

In a certain sense Marx bears a resemblance to Wycliffe. Like the English priest, the technologies necessary for the adoption of his ideas were unavailable during his own era. Just as a mass-produced vernacular Bible was impossible in a world without moveable metal type, so was any attempt at communism within the limits of the Second Disruption. Dependent on scarce fossil fuels, global living standards like those of the very wealthiest would spell environmental catastrophe, while under conditions of scarcity of both physical and cognitive labour, the pursuit of leisure for some necessarily depended on making others work harder. Yet this is now changing. Indeed, it has been for some time.

More than half a century would pass between the arrival of modern print, traditionally viewed as the publication of the Gutenberg Bible in the 1450s, and the starting gun of the Reformation with Luther's 95 Theses. While the Gutenberg press was profoundly disruptive, it only led to social transformation once it became so mundane that a little-known theologian could have his ideas printed by people he had never met and, in a matter of months, discover an audience of millions.

The same is now true for the principal technologies of the Third Disruption. These are now taking centre stage after continuous progress since the 1950s – the decade photovoltaic cells were developed, the first silicon transistor invented and DNA finally modelled. By the early 1960s the first LEDs were being experimented with, and in the 1970s so too were lithium batteries. Only now are these innovations bringing extreme supply to information, labour and resources. In so doing, they undermine two core presumptions about capitalism: firstly, that scarcity will always exist; and secondly, that goods will not be produced if their marginal cost is zero. They are – and conventional economics can't explain it.

None of the technologies at the heart of the Third Disruption are new. Rather, as with the late fifteenth century, they have quietly moved from the fringes of social life to its centre – all while riding the dividends of the experience curve and exponential growth. What happens next, however, and how these technologies are woven into the fabric of modernity, is our responsibility. There is no necessary reason why they should liberate us, or maintain our planet's ecosystems, any more than they should lead to ever-widening income inequality and widespread collapse. The direction we take next won't be the result of a predictive algorithm or unicorn startup – it will be the result of politics. The binding decisions on all of us that we collectively choose to make.

FALC Is a Beginning, Not a Destination

The shifts outlined as central to the Third Disruption are not a destination, but a beginning. FALC is not a blueprint for a steady-state Eden – those always prove disappointing anyway. Nor is it a place beyond sadness or pain, where conflict and vulnerability are consigned to the past. Pride, greed and envy will abide as long as we do, the management of discord between humans – the essence of politics – an inevitable feature of any society we share with one another. Instead, FALC is a figurehead of possibility forged for a world changing so rapidly that new utopias are needed – because the old ones no longer make sense.

Isaac Deutscher once wrote 'socialism is not evolution's last and perfect product or the end of history, but in a sense only the beginning'. This is how FALC is perhaps best conceived. It is a map by which we escape the labyrinth of scarcity and a society built on jobs; the platform from which we can begin to answer the most difficult question of all, of what it means, as Keynes once put it, to live 'wisely and agreeably and well'.

Of course, any effective map must instruct its user about immediate next steps, the clarity of which must be as apparent as the intended destination. It is for this reason that FALC demurs from idealism or an overly optimistic view of human nature, offering immediate action instead. While FALC is situated within a transformation as seismic as that of the arrival of agriculture, its concrete politics consist in specific, readily identifiable demands: a break with neoliberalism, a shift towards worker-owned production, a state–financed transition to renewable energy and universal services – rightly identified as human rights – placed beyond commodity exchange and profit.

FALC is not a manifesto for the starry-eyed poets. Rather it is born from the recognition of an increasingly obvious truth: amid the changes of the Third Disruption the 'fact' of scarcity is moving from inevitable certainty to political imposition.

This is not a book about the future but about a present that goes unacknowledged. The outline of a world immeasurably better than our own, more equal, prosperous, and creative, is there to see if only we dare to look. But insight alone is not enough. We must have the courage – for that is what is required – to argue, persuade, and build.

There is a world to win.

Bibliography

Introduction

Doug

Amazon. 'Introducing Amazon Go and the World's Most Advanced Shopping Technology'. *YouTube.com*, 5 December 2016.

Clifford, Catherine. 'Mark Cuban: The World's First Trillionaire Will Be an Artificial Intelligence Entrepreneur.' *CNBC*, 13 March 2017.

Golson, Jordan. 'Tesla Built a Huge Solar Energy Plant on the Island of Kauai'. *The Verge*, 8 March 2017.

Rosenblum, Andrew. 'A Biohacker's Plan to Upgrade Dalmatians Ends Up in the Doghouse'. *MIT Technology Review*, 1 February 2017.

'Space Act Of 2015 Passes in the House (H.R. 2262)'. *Planetary Resources*, 14 July 2015.

'Wisconsin Board Clears Way For $3 Billion Foxconn Deal'. *Reuters*, 8 November 2017.

Part I. Chaos under Heaven

1. The Great Divide

Fukuyama, Francis. 'The End of History'. *National Interest*, 16 Summer 1989.

Capitalist Realism

Cox, Christoph, Molly Whalen and Alain Badiou. 'On Evil: An Interview with Alain Badiou'. *Cabinet*, Winter 2001-2.

Fisher, Mark. *Capitalist Realism: Is There No Alternative?* Zero Books, 2010.

Menand, Louis. 'Francis Fukuyama Postpones the End of History'. *New Yorker*, 3 September 2018.

Crisis Unleashed

'Depression Looms as Global Crisis'. *BBC News*, 2 September 2009.

Hertle, Hans-Hermann and Maria Nooke. *The Victims at the Berlin Wall 1961–1989: A Biographical Handbook*. Links Verlag, 2011.

'IOM Counts 3,771 Migrant Fatalities in Mediterranean in 2015'. *International Organization for Migration*, 1 May 2016.

Jones, Owen. 'Suicide and Silence: Why Depressed Men Are Dying for Somebody to Talk To'. *Guardian*, 15 August 2014.

2008: Return of History

Allen, Katie and Larry Elliott. 'UK Joins Greece At Bottom of Wage Growth League'. *Guardian*, 27 July 2016.

Bastani, Aaron. 'Property Owning Democracy'. *LRB Blog*, 2 March 2017.

Boyce, Lee and Press Association. 'How 17m Adults Have Less Than £100 Saved for a Rainy Day'. *ThisIsMoney.co.uk*, 29 September 2016.

Butler, Patrick. 'Report Reveals Scale of Food Bank Use in the UK'. *Guardian*, 29 May 2017.

———. 'Record 60% Of Britons in Poverty Are in Working Families'. *Guardian*, 22 May 2017.

Evans, Judith. 'Home Ownership in England Falls To 30-year Low'. *Financial Times*, 2 March 2017.

Gopal, Prashant. 'Homeownership Rate in the U.S. Drops to Lowest Since 1965'. *Bloomberg News*, 28 July 2016.

McGrath, Maggie. '63% Of Americans Don't Have Enough Savings to Cover A $500 Emergency'. *Forbes*, 6 January 2016.

Noack, Rick. 'Here's How the Islamic State Compares with Real States'. *Washington Post*, 12 September 2014.

Pflaum, Nadia. 'Trump: 43 million Americans on food stamps'. *Politifact,* 21 July 2016.

Wark, McKenzie. *The Beach Beneath the Street.* Verso Books, 2017.

Measuring Inertia

Allen, Katie. 'Chinese Growth Slips to Slowest Pace For 26 Years'. *Guardian,* 20 January 2017.

Burgen, Stephen. 'Spain Youth Unemployment Reaches Record 56.1%'. *Guardian,* 30 August 2013.

'Donald Trump's Election Victory Speech: Read the Full Transcript'. *Sky News,* 9 November 2016.

'Greece Unemployment Hits a Record 25% in July'. *BBC News,* 11 October 2012.

Jackson, Gavin and Sarah O'Connor. '"Lost Decade" For UK Workers as Productivity Falls Beneath 2007 Level'. *Financial Times,* 5 July 2017.

Peck, Tom. 'Nigel Farage's Triumphalist Brexit Speech Crossed the Borders of Decency'. *Independent,* 24 June 2016.

Safi, Michael. 'India's Slowing Growth Blamed on "Big Mistake" Of Demonetisation'. *Guardian,* 1 June 2017.

York, Stephen. 'Greenspan Says Crisis Left Him in "Shocked Disbelief"'. *Independent,* 24 October 2008.

2. The Three Disruptions

Industry: The Second Disruption

Brynjolfsson, Erik and Andrew McAfee. *The Second Machine Age: Work, Progress, and Prosperity in a Time of Brilliant Technologies.* W.W. Norton, 2014.

Hobsbawm Eric. *The Age of Revolution: Europe 1789–1848.* Abacus, 2014.

Capitalism's Critics

Gawenda, Alex and Ashok Kumar. 'Made In Post-China™'. *Counterpunch,* 14 June 2013.

Harvey, David. *A Companion to Marx's Capital.* Verso Books, 2012.

Marx, Karl and Friedrich Engels. *The Communist Manifesto.* Penguin Books, 2015.

Information Unbound: The Third Disruption

Crew, Bec. 'NASA Just Fast-Tracked Its Mission to Explore a $10,000 Quadrillion Metal Asteroid'. *Sciencealert.com*, 25 May 2017.

Goodall, Chris. *The Switch: How Solar, Storage and New Tech Means Cheap Power for All*. Profile Books, 2016.

Going Exponential: Ibn Khallikan to Kodak

Brynjolfsson, Erik and Andrew McAfee. *The Second Machine Age: Work, Progress, and Prosperity in a Time of Brilliant Technologies*. W.W. Norton, 2014.

Chace, Calum. *The Economic Singularity: Artificial Intelligence and the Death of Capitalism*. Three Cs Publishing, 2016.

Moore, G.E. 'Cramming More Components onto Integrated Circuits'. *Proceedings of the IEEE*, 1998.

Pickover, Clifford. *The Math Book: From Pythagoras to the 57th Dimension, 250 Milestones in the History of Mathematics*. Sterling, 2012.

Can Moore's Law Endure?

L.S. 'The End of Moore's Law'. *Economist*, 19 April 2015.

More Than Processing

Coughlin, Tom. 'Toshiba's 3-D Magnetic Recording May Increase Hard Disk Drive Capacity', *Forbes*, 9 July 2015.

Komorowski, Matt. 'A History of Storage Cost'. *Mkomo.com*, 9 March 2014.

Service, Robert. 'DNA Could Store All of the World's Data in One Room'. *Science*, 2 March 2017.

The Power of Experience

Goodall, Chris. *The Switch: How Solar, Storage and New Tech Means Cheap Power for All*. Profile Books, 2016.

'The Experience Curve'. *Economist*, 14 September 2009.

From Crisis to Utopia

Levy, Steven. 'Hackers at 30: "Hackers" and "Information Wants to Be Free"'. *Wired*, 21 November 2014.

Marx, Karl. *Grundrisse*. Penguin, 1993.

3. What Is Fully Automated Luxury Communism?

Future Shock 1858

Cyert, Richard M. and David C. Mowery, eds. *Technology and Employment: Innovation and Growth in the US Economy*. National Academy of Sciences, 1987.

Marx, Karl. *Grundrisse*. Penguin, 1993.

Communism: A World beyond Scarcity

Marx, Karl. *Capital: Volume 3*. Penguin Books, 1993.

Marx, Karl. *Critique of the Gotha Programme*. Progress Publishers, 1960.

Post-Capitalism without Communism: J. M. Keynes

Allen, Katie and Larry Elliott. 'UK Joins Greece At Bottom of Wage Growth League'. *Guardian*, 27 July 2016.

Corlett, Adam, Stephen Clarke and Torsten Bell. 'Public and Family Finances Squeezes Extended Well Into the 2020s By Grim Budget Forecasts'. *Resolution Foundation*, 9 March 2017.

Keynes, John Maynard. *Essays in Persuasion*. Cambridge University Press, 2013.

Taylor, Ciaren, Andrew Jowett and Michael Hardie. 'An Examination of Falling Real Wages, 2010 – 2013'. *Office for National Statistics*, 31 January 2014.

Turchin, Peter. 'The End of Prosperity: Why Did Real Wages Stop Growing in the 1970s?' *Evolution Institute*, 4 April 2013.

Post-Capitalism and Information: Peter Drucker

Drucker, Peter. *Post-Capitalist Society*. Butterworth-Heinemann, 1998.

Marx, Karl. *A Contribution To the Critique of Political Economy*. Progress Publishers, 1977.

Taylorism and the Productivity Revolution

Drucker, Peter. *Post-Capitalist Society*. Butterworth-Heinemann, 1998.

Marx, Karl. *Grundrisse*. Penguin, 1993.

Information Goods Want to Be Free – Really

DeLong, J. Bradford and Lawrence Summers. 'The "New Economy": Background, Historical Perspective, Questions, and Speculations'. *Economic Review, Federal Reserve Bank of Kansas City*, 2001.

Romer, Paul. 'Endogenous Technological Change'. *Journal of Political Economy*, 1990.

Part II. New Travellers

4. Full Automation: Post-Scarcity in Labour

When Capital Becomes Labour

'Ford Factory Workers Get 40-Hour Week'. *History.com*, 2009.

N. V. 'Difference Engine: Luddite Legacy'. *Economist*, 4 November 2011.

Peak Horse

Groom, Brian. 'The Wisdom of Horse Manure'. *Financial Times*, 2 September 2013.

Peak Human

Bloodgate, Henry. 'CEO of Apple Partner Foxconn: "Managing One Million Animals Gives Me A Headache"'. *Business Insider*, 19 January 2012.

Coco, Federica. 'Most US Manufacturing Jobs Lost to Technology, Not Trade'. *Financial Times*, 2 December 2016.

Dasgupta, Skit and Ajith Singh. 'Will Services Be the New Engine of Indian Economic Growth?' *Development and Change*, 2005.

'Industrial Metamorphosis'. *Economist*, 29 September 2005.

Kilby, Emily R. 'The Demographics of the US Equine Population'. In *The State of the Animals*. Edited by D.J. Salem and A.N. Rowan. Humane Society Press, 2007. pp. 175–205.

Markoff, John. 'New Wave of Deft Robots Is Changing Global Industry'. *New York Times*, 19 August 2012.

National Research Council. *The Long-Term Impact of Technology on Employment and Unemployment*. National Academies Press, 1983.

Perez, Bien. 'Annual Robotics Spending in China to Reach US $59b by 2020'. *South China Morning Post*, 4 April 2017.

Rifkin, Jeremy. 'Return of a Conundrum'. *Guardian*, 2 March 2004.

——. *The Zero Marginal Cost Society*. Palgrave Macmillan, 2014.

Taylor, Ciaren, Andrew Jowett and Michael Hardie. 'An Examination of Falling Real Wages, 2010 – 2013'. *Office for National Statistics*, 31 January 2014.

Wallop, Harry. 'Manufacturing Jobs to Fall to Lowest Level Since 1841'. *Telegraph*, 6 February 2009.

Zoo, Mandy. 'Rise of the Robots: 60,000 Workers Culled from Just One Factory as China's Struggling Electronics Hub Turns to Artificial Intelligence'. *South China Morning Post*, 21 May 2016.

The End of Mass Agriculture

International Labour Organization. 'Employment in Industry (% of Total Employment) (Modelled ILO Estimate)'. *World Bank*, November 2017.

'Labor Force – by Occupation'. *CIA World Factbook*, 2009.

Riser, Max. 'Employment in Agriculture'. *Our World in Data*, 2018.

UN Food and Agriculture Organization (FAO). Statistics from 2018. fao.org/faostat/en/#data/countries_by_commodity/visualize

Rise of the Robots

Campbell, Murray, A. Joseph Hoane Jr. and Feng-Hsiung Hsu. 'Deep Blue'. *Artificial Intelligence* 134: 1–2 (January 2002).

Jennings, Ken. 'My Puny Human Brain'. *Slate*, 16 February 2011.

Moravec, Hans. *Mind Children: The Future of Robot and Human Intelligence*. Harvard University Press, 1988.

Atlas Somersaults

Thomson, Iain. 'Atlas Unplugged! Darpa's Unterminator Robot Cuts the Power Cable'. *Register*, 23 January 2015.

Autonomous Vehicles

Balakrishnan, Anita. 'Drivers Could Lose up to 25,000 Jobs per Month when Self-Driving Cars Hit, Goldman Sachs Says'. *CNBC*, 22 May 2017.

Bomey, Nathan. 'US Vehicle Deaths Topped 40,000 in 2017, National Safety Council Estimates'. *USA Today*, 15 February 2018.

Darter, Michael. 'DARPA's Debacle in the Desert'. *Popular Science*, 4 June 2004.

Dillow, Clay. 'Revealed: Google's Car Fleet Has Been Driving around

Unmanned for 140,000 Miles Already'. *Popular Science*, 11 October 2010.

Ford, Martin. *The Rise of the Robots: Technology and the Threat of Mass Unemployment*. Oneworld, 2017.

Marshall, Aarian. 'As Uber Flails, Its Self-driving Car Research Rolls On'. *Wired*, 23 June 2017.

Thrun, Sebastian. 'What We're Driving At'. *Official Google Blog*, 9 October 2010.

Technological Unemployment Is Coming

Ahmed, Kamal. '900,000 UK Retail Jobs Could Be Lost by 2025, Warns BRC'. *BBC*, 29 February 2016.

Amazon. 'Introducing Amazon Go and the World's Most Advanced Shopping Technology'. *YouTube.com*, 5 December 2016.

Armstrong, Ashley. 'Chinese Online Retailer JD Plans to Open Hundreds of Unmanned Shops, Ahead of Amazon'. *Telegraph*, 14 December 2017.

Chace, Calum. *The Economic Singularity: Artificial Intelligence and the Death of Capitalism*. Three Cs Publishing, 2016.

Clifford, Catherine. 'Mark Cuban: The World's First Trillionaire Will Be an Artificial Intelligence Entrepreneur.' *CNBC*, 13 March 2017.

Elliott, Larry. 'Robots Threaten 15m UK Jobs, Says Bank of England's Chief Economist'. *Guardian*, 12 November 2015.

'Future Work/Technology 2050'. *Millennium Project*, 1 December 2014.

Nasiripour, Shahien. 'White House Predicts Robots May Take Over Many Jobs That Pay $20 per Hour'. *Huffington Post*, 24 February 2016.

Statt, Nick. 'Amazon's Cashier-Free Go Stores May Only Need Six Human Employees', *The Verge*, 6 February 2017.

Taylor, Ciaren, Andrew Jowett and Michael Hardie. 'An Examination of Falling Real Wages, 2010 – 2013'. *Office for National Statistics*, 31 January 2014.

Thibodeau, Patrick. 'One in Three Jobs Will Be Taken by Software or Robots by 2025'. *Computer World*. 6 October 2014.

Thompson, Alexandra. '"Robot Surgery" Could Save Men from

Prostate Cancer'. *Daily Mail*, 24 November 2017.

Turner, Nick, Selina Wang and Spencer Soper. 'Amazon to Acquire Whole Foods for $13.7 Billion'. *Bloomberg*, 16 June 2017.

Williams-Grut, Oscar. 'Mark Carney: "Every Technological Revolution Mercilessly Destroys Jobs Well Before the New Ones Emerge"'. *Business Insider*, 6 December 2016.

Actually Existing Automation

Marr, Bernard. 'First FDA Approval for Clinical Cloud-Based Deep Learning in Healthcare'. *Forbes*, 20 January 2017.

Croft, Jane. 'More than 100,000 Legal Roles to Become Automated'. *Financial Times*, 15 March 2016.

Snow, Jackie. 'A New Algorithm Can Spot Pneumonia Better than a Radiologist'. *MIT Technology Review*, 16 November 2017.

The Future of Work

Brynjolfsson, Erik and Andrew McAfee. *The Second Machine Age: Work, Progress, and Prosperity in a Time of Brilliant Technologies.* W.W. Norton, 2014.

5. Limitless Power: Post-Scarcity in Energy

Energy and Disruption

Malm, Andreas. *Fossil Capital: The Rise of Steam Power and the Roots of Global Warming.* Verso Books, 2016.

Arrival of the Anthropocene

Lynch, Patrick. 'Secrets from the Past Point to Rapid Climate Change in the Future'. *NASA*, 14 December 2011.

Can We Survive Climate Catastrophe?

Klein, Naomi. *This Changes Everything: Capitalism vs. the Climate.* Penguin Books, 2015.

Lynas, Mark. *Six Degrees: Our Future on a Hotter Planet.* Fourth Estate, 2007.

Energy Wants to Be Free

Goodall, Chris. *The Switch: How Solar, Storage and New Tech Means Cheap Power for All,* Profile Books, 2016.

Watts, Jonathan. 'We Have 12 Years to Limit Climate Change Catastrophe, Warns UN'. *Guardian*, 8 October 2018.

Solar Energy: Limitless, Clean, Free
Diamandis, Peter and Steven Kotler. *Abundance: The Future Is Better than You Think*. Free Press, 2014.

A Quiet Revolution
'Electricity Generation Mix by Quarter and Fuel Source (GB)'. *UK Office of Gas and Electricity Markets*, October 2018.
Goodall, Chris. *The Switch: How Solar, Storage and New Tech Means Cheap Power for All*, Profile Books, 2016.
Hanley, Steve. 'New PPA in Arizona Locks in Lowest Solar Prices in US as Demise of Navajo Station Looms'. *Clean Technica*, 11 June 2018.
McGreevy, Ronan. 'Scotland "on Target" for 100% Renewable Energy by 2020'. *Irish Times*, 4 November 2017.
'Onshore Wind Power Now as Affordable as Any Other Source, Solar to Halve by 2020'. *IRENA*, 13 January 2018.
Vaughan, Adam. 'Time to Shine: Solar Power Is Fastest-growing Source of New Energy'. *Guardian*, 4 October 2017.

Racing to the Future
Asthana, Anushka and Matthew Taylor. 'Britain to Ban Sale of All Diesel and Petrol Cars and Vans from 2040'. *Guardian*, 25 July 2017.
Dorrier, Jason. 'Solar Is Now the Cheapest Energy There Is in the Sunniest Parts of the World'. *Singularity Hub*, 18 May 2017.
Goodall, Chris. *The Switch: How Solar, Storage and New Tech Means Cheap Power for All*, Profile Books, 2016.
Penn, Ivan. 'Cheaper Battery Is Unveiled as a Step to a Carbon-Free Grid'. *New York Times*, 26 September 2018.

Solar and the Global Switch
Chao, Rebecca. 'Libya Uses World's First Mobile Voter Registration System for Parliament Elections'. *Tech President*, 25 June 2014.
Goodall, Chris. *The Switch: How Solar, Storage and New Tech Means Cheap Power for All*, Profile Books, 2016.

McKibben, Bill. 'The Race to Solar-Power Africa'. *New Yorker*, 26 June 2017.

Poushter, Jacob. 'Cell Phones in Africa: Communication Lifeline'. *Pew Global Research*, 15 April 2015.

'Reducing Risks, Promoting Healthy Life'. *World Health Organization*, 2002.

T.S. 'Why Does Kenya Lead the World in Mobile Money?' *Economist*, 2 March 2015.

Tricarico, Daniele. 'Case Study: Vodafone Turkey Farmers' Club'. *GSM Association*, June 2015.

Vaughan, Adam. 'Time to Shine: Solar Power Is Fastest-growing Source of New Energy'. *Guardian*, 4 October 2017.

Wind

Davies, Rob. 'Wind Turbines "Could Supply Most of UK's Electricity"'. *Guardian*, 8 November 2016.

'*The Guardian* View of Offshore Wind: Cheaper and Greener'. *Guardian*, 13 September 2017.

Harrabin, Roger. 'Offshore Wind Power Cheaper than New Nuclear'. *BBC News*, 11 September 2017.

Rifkin, Jeremy. *The Zero Marginal Cost Society*. Palgrave Macmillan, 2014.

Tamblyn, Thomas. 'Amazingly, Wind Farms Provided Double the Energy Needed to Power All of Scotland in October'. *Huffington Post*, 7 November 2017.

Vaughan, Adam. 'Nuclear Plans Should Be Rethought after Fall in Offshore Windfarm Costs'. *Guardian*, 11 September 2017.

Vaughan, Adam. 'UK Wind Power Overtakes Coal for First Time'. *Guardian*, 6 January 2017.

Keeping Warm

'Dramatic Jump in Excess Winter Deaths'. *Age UK*, 22 November 2017.

Goodall, Chris. *The Switch: How Solar, Storage and New Tech Means Cheap Power for All*. Profile Books, 2016.

Huck, Nichole. '"Passive Home" Movement a Success in Germany, but Not in Saskatchewan Where It Started'. *CBC News*, 5 August 2015.

The Solutions to Climate Change Are Here
Rifkin, Jeremy. 'Capitalism Is Making Way for the Age of Free'. *Guardian*, 31 March 2014.

6. Mining the Sky: Post-Scarcity in Resources

Finite World
Ahmed, Nafeez. 'Exhaustion of Cheap Mineral Resources Is Terraforming Earth – Scientific Report'. *Guardian*, 4 June 2014.
Withnall, Adam. 'Britain Has Only 100 Harvests Left in Its Farm Soil as Scientists Warn of Growing "Agricultural Crisis"'. *Independent*, 20 October 2014.

Asteroid Mining
Ludacer, Rob and Jessica Orwig. 'SpaceX Is about to Launch Its Monster Mars Rocket for the First Time – Here's How It Stacks Up Against Other Rockets'. *Business Insider*, 4 January 2018.
SpaceX. 'SpaceX Interplanetary Transport System'. *YouTube.com*, 27 September 2016.

Birth of a Private Space Industry
End, Rae Botsford. 'Rocket Lab: The Electron, the Rutherford, and Why Peter Beck Started It in the First Place'. *Spaceflight Insider*, 2 May 2015.
Spacevidcast. 'SpaceX Reaches Orbit with Falcon 1 – Flight 4 (Full Video Including Elon Musk Statement)'. *Youtube.com*, 28 September 2008.
SpaceX. 'Orbcomm-2 Full Launch Webcast'. *YouTube.com*, 21 December 2015.
Vance, Ashlee. *Elon Musk: How the Billionaire CEO of SpaceX and Tesla Is Shaping Our Future*. Virgin Digital, 2015.

Falling Costs, Rising Ambitions
'Apollo Program Budget Appropriations'. *NASA*.
Dorrier, Jason. 'Risk Takers Are Back in the Space Race – and That's a Good Thing'. *Singularity Hub*, 17 August 2017.
Erwin, Sandra. 'Rocket Startup Sees Big Future in Military Launch'. *Space News*, 1 July 2018.

Gush, Loren. 'Rocket Lab Will Launch Its Small Experimental Rocket Again this December'. *The Verge*, 29 November 2017.

Knapp, Alex. 'Rocket Lab Becomes a Space Unicorn with a $75 Million Funding Round'. *Forbes*, 21 March 2017.

Lo, Bernie and Nyshka Chandran. 'Rocket Lab Nears Completion of World's First Private Orbital Launch Site in New Zealand'. *CNBC*, 28 August 2016.

'Rocket Lab Reveals First Battery-Powered Rocket for Commercial Launches to Space'. *Rocket Lab USA*, 31 May 2015.

Pielke, Roger, Jr. and Radford Byerly, Jr. 'The Space Shuttle Program: Performance versus Promise'. *Space Policy Alternatives*, Westview Press, 1992.

Vance, Ashlee. 'These Giant Printers Are Meant to Make Rockets'. *Bloomberg News*, 18 October 2017.

Moon Express

'The Global Exploration Strategy: The Framework for Coordination'. *NASA*, 31 May 2007.

Grush, Loren. 'To Mine the Moon, Private Company Moon Express Plans to Build a Fleet of Robotic Landers'. *The Verge*, 12 July 2017.

MoonExpress.com

The Province of All Mankind

Cookson, Clive. 'Luxembourg Launches Plan to Mine Asteroids for Minerals'. *Financial Times*, 2 February 2016.

Dorrier, Jason. 'Risk Takers Are Back in the Space Race – and That's a Good Thing'. *Singularity Hub*, 17 August 2017.

Fernholz, Tim. 'Space Is not a "Global Commons," Top Trump Space Official Says'. *Quartz*, 19 December 2017.

Hennigan, W.J. 'MoonEx Aims to Scour Moon for Rare Materials'. *Los Angeles Times*, 8 April 2011.

Marx, Karl. 'Chapter 44: Differential Rent Also on the Worst Cultivated Soil'. *Marxists.org*.

Orphanides, K.G. 'American Companies Could Soon Mine Asteroids for Profit'. *Wired*, 12 November 2015.

'Outer Space Treaty'. *US Department of State*.

'Reopening the American Frontier: Exploring How the Outer Space

Treaty Will Impact American Commerce and Settlement in Space'. *US Senate Committee on Commerce, Science and Transportation*, 23 May 2017.

Beyond the Limits of the Earth

Chamberlin, Alan B. 'All known Near Earth Asteroids (NEA), Cumulative Discoveries over Time'. *NASA Jet Propulsion Laboratory*, 15 January 2013. Deepspaceindustries.com

Edwards, Jim. 'Goldman Sachs: Space-Mining for Platinum Is "More Realistic Than Perceived"'. *Business Insider*, 6 April 2017.

Herridge, Linda. 'OSIRIS-REx Prepared for Mapping, Sampling Mission to Asteroid Bennu'. *NASA*, 6 August 2017.

Lewis, John. *Mining the Sky: Untold Riches from the Asteroids, Comets, and Planets*. Basic Books, 1997.

Malik, Tariq. 'Asteroid Dust Successfully Returned by Japanese Space Probe'. *Space.com*, 16 November 2010.

Müller, T.G. et al. 'Hayabusa-2 Mission Target Asteroid 162173 Ryugu (1999 JU3): Searching for the Object's Spin-Axis Orientation'. *Astronomy & Astrophysics*, March 2017.

Planetaryresources.com

Wall, Mike. 'Asteroid Mining May Be a Reality by 2025'. *Space.com*, 11 August 2015.

Yongliao, Zou. 'China's Deep-Space Exploration to 2030'. *Chinese Journal of Space Science*, 2014.

The Scramble for Space

Brophy, John et al. 'Asteroid Retrieval Feasibility Study'. *Keck Institute for Space Studies*, April 2012.

Edwards, Jim. 'Goldman Sachs: Space-Mining for Platinum Is "More Realistic Than Perceived"'. *Business Insider*, 6 April 2017.

Abundance beyond Value

'1974 NASA Authorization Hearings, Ninety-third Congress, First Session, on H.R. 4567 (superseded by H.R. 7528)'. *US Government Printing Office*, 1973.

Dorrier, Jason. 'Risk Takers Are Back in the Space Race – and That's a Good Thing'. *Singularity Hub*, 17 August 2017.

Eisenhower, Dwight D. 'Address Before the 15th General Assembly of the United Nations, New York City'. *The American Presidency Project.*

'Protocol on Environmental Protection to the Antarctic Treaty'. *Atlantic Treaty Secretariat*, 4 October 1991.

Scotti, Monique. 'NASA Plans Mission to a Metal-rich Asteroid Worth Quadrillions'. *Global News*, 12 January 2017.

7. Editing Destiny

An Ageing Species

'Are You Ready? What You Need to Know About Ageing'. *World Health Organization*, 2012.

'Demographics and Markets: The Effects of Ageing'. *Financial Times*, 25 October 2016.

Lawrence, Mathew. 'Future Proof: Britain in the 2020s'. *Institute for Public Policy Research*, December 2016.

Mrsnik, Marko. 'Global Aging 2013: Rising To The Challenge'. *Standard & Poor's*, 20 March 2013.

Mrsnik, Marko. 'Global Aging 2016: 58 Shades of Gray'. *Standard & Poor's*, 28 April 2016.

'People and Possibilities in a World of 7 Billion.' *United Nations Population Fund*, 2011.

Pomeranz, Kenneth. *The Great Divergence: China, Europe, and the Making of the Modern World Economy.* Princeton University Press, 2000.

Prentice, Thomson. 'Health, History and Hard Choices: Funding Dilemmas in a Fast-Changing World'. *World Health Organization*, August 2006.

'World Population Projected to Reach 9.6 Billion by 2050'. *UN News*, 13 June 2013.

Ageing in Britain: Austerity beyond Austerity

'Dementia Now Leading Cause of Death'. *BBC News*, 14 November 2016.

Gallagher, James. 'Dementia Cases "Set to Treble Worldwide" by

2050'. *BBC News*, 5 December 2013.

Lain, Douglas. *Advancing Conversations: Aubrey De Grey – Advocate for An Indefinite Human Lifespan*. Zero Books, 2016.

Marcus, Mary Brophy. 'The Top 10 Leading Causes of Death in the US'. *CBS News*, 30 June 2016.

(Genetic) Information Wants to Be Free

'An Overview of the Human Genome Project'. *National Human Genome Research Institute*, November 8, 2012.

Buhr, Sarah. 'Illumina Wants to Sequence Your Whole Genome for $100'. *Tech Crunch*, 10 January 2017.

Nowogrodzki, Anna. 'Should Babies Have Their Genomes Sequenced?' *MIT Technology Review*, 2 July 2015.

Pennisi, Elizabeth. 'Biologists Propose to Sequence the DNA of All Life on Earth'. *Science*, 24 February 2017.

Sieh, W. 'The Role of Genome Sequencing in Personalized Breast Cancer Prevention'. *Cancer Epidemiology, Biomarkers and Prevention*, November 2014.

Singularity University Summits. 'The Biotechnology Century | Raymond McCauley | Singularity University Global Summit'. *YouTube.com*, 21 April 2017.

Venter, Craig. *A Life Decoded: My Genome, My Life*. Viking, 2007.

Yong, Ed. 'Fighting Ebola With a Palm-Sized DNA Sequencer'. *The Atlantic*, 16 September 2015.

Extreme Supply in Healthcare: Gene Therapies

Beall, Abigail. 'Genetically-modified Humans: What Is CRISPR and How Does It Work?' *Wired*, 5 February 2017.

'CRISPR Reverses Huntington's Disease in Mice'. *Genetic Engineering and Biotechnology News*, 20 June 2017.

'CRISPR Timeline'. *Broad Institute*.

Cyranoski, David. 'CRISPR Gene Editing Tested in a Person'. *Nature*, 24 November 2016. pp. 479.

Molteni, Megan. 'Everything You Need to Know About Crispr Gene Editing'. *Wired*, 5 December 2017.

Regalado, Antonio. 'First Gene-Edited Dogs Reported in China'. *MIT Technology Review*, 19 October 2015.

Rosenblum, Andrew. 'A Biohacker's Plan to Upgrade Dalmatians Ends Up in the Doghouse'. *MIT Technology Review*, 1 February 2017.

Singularity University Summits. 'The Biotechnology Century | Raymond McCauley | Singularity University Global Summit'. *YouTube.com*, 21 April 2017.

Stapleton, Andrew. 'Scientists Have Used CRISPR to Slow The Spread of Cancer Cells'. *Science Alert*, 1 June 2017.

Yu, Alan. 'How a Gene Editing Tool Went from Labs to a Middle-School Classroom'. *NPR*, 27 May 2017.

Welcome to Elysium

'Alan Kurdi | 100 Photographs | The Most Influential Images of All Time'. *Time*.

de Selding, Peter B. 'SpaceX's Reusable Falcon 9: What Are the Real Cost Savings for Customers?' *Space News*, 25 April 2016.

8. Food Without Animals

Food, Surplus and Disruptions

Pearce, Fred. 'The Sterile Banana'. *Conservation*, 26 September 2008.

Zohary, Daniel, Maria Hopf and Ehud Weiss. *Domestication of Plants in the Old World: The Origin and Spread of Domesticated Plants in Southwest Asia, Europe, and the Mediterranean Basin*. Oxford University Press, 2012.

A Stretching World

Arsenault, Chris. 'Only 60 Years of Farming Left If Soil Degradation Continues'. *Scientific American*, 5 December 2014.

Brown, Lester. *Plan B 3.0: Mobilizing to Save Civilization*. W.W. Norton, 2009.

Carrington, Damian. 'Earth's Sixth Mass Extinction Event Under Way, Scientists Warn'. *Guardian*, 10 July 2017.

Howard, Emma. 'Humans Have Already Used Up 2015's Supply of Earth's Resources – Analysis'. *Guardian*, 12 August 2015.

Jevons, William. *The Coal Question*. 1865.

Lynas, Mark. *Six Degrees: Our Future on a Hotter Planet*. Fourth Estate, 2007.

Malthus, Thomas. *An Essay on the Principle of Population*. 1798.

Myers, Ransom A. and Boris Worm. 'Rapid Worldwide Depletion of Predatory Fish Communities'. *Nature*, 15 May 2003.

Nelson, Gerald C. et al. *Food Security, Farming, and Climate Change to 2050: Scenarios, Results, Policy Options*. International Food Policy Research Institute, 2010.

'World Must Sustainably Produce 70 Percent More Food by Mid-Century – UN Report'. *UN News*, 3 December 2013.

Food as Information: The Green Revolution

'Agricultural Land (% of Land Area)'. *World Bank*, 28 September 2017.

Chambers, Ian and John Humble. *Plan for the Planet: A Business Plan for a Sustainable World*. Gower, 2012.

De Datta, S.K. et al. 'Effect of Plant Type and Nitrogen Level on the Growth Characteristics and Grain Yield of Indica Rice in the Tropics'. *Agronomy Journal*, 1968.

Ehrlich, Paul, *The Population Bomb*. Sierra Club/Ballantine Books, 1968.

'Prevalence of Undernourishment (% of Population)'. *World Bank*, 28 September 2017.

Swaminathan, M.S. 'Obituary: Norman E. Borlaug (1914–2009) Plant Scientist Who Transformed Global Food Production'. *Nature*, 2009. pp. 461.

Completing the Green Revolution

Easterbrook, Gregg. 'Forgotten Benefactor of Humanity'. *Atlantic*, January 1997.

Synthetic Meat: Meat without Animals

Caughill, Patrick. 'The Future of Protein: Here's How Lab-Grown Meat Is Transforming Our Future'. *Futurism*, 19 January 2017.

Cow Weight FAQ. *Pro B Farms*. http://www.probfarms.com/layout_images/fs-cowweight.pdf.

Gold, Mark. *The Global Benefits of Eating Less Meat*. Compassion in World Farming Trust, 2004.

'Rearing Cattle Produces More Greenhouse Gases than Driving Cars, UN Report Warns'. *UN News,* 29 November 2006.

Reijnders, Lucas and Sam Soret. 'Quantification of the Environmental Impact Of Different Dietary Protein Choices'. *The American Journal of Clinical Nutrition,* 1 September 2003. pp. 664S–668S.

Vidal, John. '10 Ways Vegetarianism Can Help Save the Planet'. *Guardian,* 18 July 2010.

'Water'. *Global Agriculture.*

'WHO World Water Day Report'. *World Health Organization,* 2001.

World Agriculture: Towards 2015/2030. Food and Agriculture Organization of the United Nations, 2003.

The $325,000 Hamburger

Card, Jon. 'Lab-Grown Food: "The Goal Is to Remove the Animal from Meat Production"'. *Guardian,* 24 July 2017.

Ceurstemont, Sandrine. 'Make Your Own Meat with Open-Source Cells – No Animals Necessary'. *New Scientist,* 11 January 2017.

Coyne, Andy. 'Just Planning to Launch Lab-Grown Chicken Product this Year'. *Just-Food,* 18 October 2018.

Heid, Markham. 'You Asked: Should I Be Nervous About Lab-Grown Meat?' *Time,* 14 September 2016.

'Indian-American Scientist Has Discovered a Way for Us to Eat Meat without Killing Animals'. *Huffington Post India,* 14 March 2016.

Jha, Alok. 'First Lab-Grown Hamburger Gets Full Marks for "Mouth Feel"'. *Guardian,* 6 August 2013.

'Lab-Grown Meat Would "Cut Emissions and Save Energy"'. *Phys Org,* 21 June 2011.

Mandelbaum, Ryan F. 'Behind the Hype of "Lab-Grown" Meat'. *Gizmodo,* 14 August 2017.

Memphis Meats. 'The World's First Cell-Based Meatball – Memphis Meats'. *Youtube.com,* 31 January 2016.

Schwartz, Ariel. 'The $325,000 Lab-Grown Hamburger Now Costs Less Than $12'. *Fast Company,* 1 April 2015.

Steinfeld, Henning et al. *Livestock's Long Shadow.* Food and Agriculture Organization of the United Nations, 2006.

Watson, Elaine. 'Cultured fish co. Finless Foods aims to achieve price parity with Bluefin tuna by the end of 2019'. *Food Navigator*, 21 December 2017.

'What Is Cultured Meat'. *Cultured Beef.*

Meat from Vegetables

Chiorando, Maria. 'JUST Vegan Egg Will be Available to Buy Online Next Month'. *Plant Based News*, 17 July 2018.

Clarafoods.com

Impossibleburger.com.

'Impossible Foods Launches Production at First Large-Scale Plant'. *Business Wire*, 7 September 2017.

Simon, Matt. 'The Impossible Burger: Inside the Strange Science of the Fake Meat That "Bleeds"'. *Wired*, 20 September 2017.

Steinfeld, Henning et al. *Livestock's Long Shadow*. Food and Agriculture Organization of the United Nations, 2006.

Tetrick, Josh. 'Meat and Seafood (But Without the Animal)'. *LinkedIn*, 27 June 2017.

Van Hemert, Kyle. 'Inside Look: The Startup Lab Using Plants to Make Next-Gen Super Eggs'. *Wired*, 10 December 2013.

Watson, Elaine. 'Perfect Day in Talks With Food Industry Partners to Commercialize Animal-Free Dairy Ingredients'. *Food Navigator*, 19 December 2017.

Champagne Socialism

Diamandis, Peter and Steven Kotler. *Abundance: The Future Is Better than You Think*. Free Press, 2014.

Dormehl, Luke. 'No Grapes Necessary — Ava Winery Makes Fine Wines Molecule by Molecule'. *Digital Trends*, 8 August 2017.

'Globetrotting Food Will Travel Farther Than Ever This Thanksgiving'. *Worldwatch Institute*.

Goldfarb, Alan. 'The Pivot to Whiskey'. *The Verge*, 23 August 2018.

Goldfield, Hannah. 'An Exclusive First Taste of Lab-Made Whiskey'. *Wall Street Journal*, 1 October 2018.

Lawrence, Felicity. 'The Supermarket Food Gamble May Be Up'. *Guardian*, 20 February 2017.

Part III. Paradise Found

9. Popular Support

Against Elite Technology

Marx, Karl. *Grundrisse*. 1857.

Rancière, Jacques. 'Attacks On "Populism" Seek to Enshrine the Idea That There is No Alternative'. *Verso Books Blog*, 2 May 2017.

Rancière, Jacques. 'The People Are Not a Brutal and Ignorant Mass'. *Verso Books Blog*, 30 January 2013.

Srincek, Nick and Alex Williams. *Inventing the Future*. Verso Books, 2016.

The Red and the Green

'Balcombe "Fracking" Village in First Solar Panel Scheme'. *BBC News*, 28 January 2015.

Brand, Stewart. 'WE ARE AS GODS'. *Whole Earth Catalog*, Fall 1968.

Against Globalism, towards Internationalism

Klein, Naomi. *This Changes Everything: Capitalism vs. the Climate*. Penguin Books, 2015.

Marx, Karl. *A Contribution to the Critique of Political Economy*. Progress Publishers, 1977.

10. Fundamental Principles

Carillion's Collapse and the East Coast Line

Bastani, Aaron. 'Britain Isn't Working'. *The New York Times*, 23 January 2018.

Boffey, Daniel. 'East Coast Mainline: Profitable and Publicly Owned – So Why Sell It?' *Guardian*, 23 October 2013.

Leach, Adam. 'UK Public Sector is World's Second-Largest Outsourcing Market'. *Chartered Institute of Procurement and Supply*, 22 March 2013.

Mason, Paul. 'Ink It Onto Your Knuckles – Carillion Is How Neoliberalism Lives and Breathes'. *Novara Media*, 15 January 2018.

McNulty, Roy. *Realising the Potential of GB Rail*. Department for Transport, May 2011.

Topham, Gwyn. 'East Coast Line Bailout Puts Rail Privatisation Back in Spotlight'. *Guardian,* 10 February 2018.

The Grenfell Fire

Osborne, Samuel and Harriet Agerholm. 'Grenfell Tower Inquiry: Refurbishment Turned Building Into "Death Trap Using Public Funds"'. *Independent,* 5 June 2018.

Stone, Jon. 'Britain Could Slash Environmental and Safety Standards "A Very Long Way" after Brexit, Tory MP Jacob Rees-Mogg Says'. *Independent,* 6 December 2016.

Ending Neoliberalism 1: The Preston Model

Chakrabortty, Aditya. 'In 2011 Preston hit Rock Bottom. Then it Took Back Control'. *Guardian,* 31 January 2018.

'The Cleveland Model—How the Evergreen Cooperatives are Building Community Wealth'. *Community Wealth,* February 2013.

Hanna, Thomas M., Joe Guinan and Joe Bilsborough. 'The "Preston Model" and the Modern Politics of Municipal Socialism'. *Open Democracy,* 12 June 2018.

Parveen, Nazia and Rachael Bunyan. 'Preston Named Best City to Live and Work in North-West England'. *Guardian,* 8 November 2016.

People's Businesses, People's Banks

Barrott, Cheryl et al. 'Alternative Models of Ownership'. *UK Labour Party,* 11 June 2017.

Clancy, John. *The Secret Wealth Garden: Re-Wiring Local Government Pension Funds back into Regional Economies.* Lulu.com, 2014.

Return of the State: UBS

Moore, Henrietta L. 'Social Prosperity for the Future: A Proposal for Universal Basic Services'. *University College London Institute for Global Prosperity,* 2017.

'NHS Statistics, Facts and Figures'. *NHS Confederation,* 14 July 2017.

Decarbonisation

Klein, Naomi. *This Changes Everything: Capitalism vs. the Climate.* Penguin Books, 2015.

'Softbank and Saudi Arabia Announce New Solar Generation Project'. *CNBC*, 27 March 2018.

11. Reforging the Capitalist State

Money for Nothing

Martinelli, Luke. 'Assessing the Case for a Universal Basic Income in the UK.' *University of Bath Institute for Policy Research*, September 2017.

Van Parijs, Philippe and Yannick Vanderborght. *Basic Income: A Radical Proposal for a Free Society and a Sane Economy*. Harvard University Press, 2017.

Zamora, Daniel. 'The Case Against a Basic Income'. *Jacobin*, 28 December 2017.

Central Banks as Central Planners

Blakely, Grace. 'On Borrowed Time: Finance and the UK's Current Account Deficit'. *Institute for Public Policy Research*, 10 July 2018.

Mason, J.W. 'Socialize Finance'. *Jacobin*, 28 November 2016.

The End of GDP

Gibbons, Kevin. 'Why Wikipedia is Top on Google: the SEO Truth No-One Wants to Hear'. *Econsulting*, 14 February 2012.

Kennedy, Robert. 'Remarks at the University of Kansas'. Speech, Lawrence, Kansas, 18 March 1968. *John F. Kennedy Presidential Library and Museum*.

Kuznets, Simon in report to the Congress, 1934. In *Globalization: Critical Perspectives*. Edited by Gernot Kohler and Emilio José Chaves, 2003.

'We'd better watch out'. *New York Times Book Review*, July 12 1987.

12. FALC

Mims, Christopher. 'The Six Laws of Technology Everyone Should Know'. *Wall Street Journal*, 26 November 2017.

Novara Media. 'Technology and Post Capitalism'. *Youtube.com*, 25 September 2017.

Futures Deferred

'How Luther Went Viral'. *Economist*, 17 December 2011.

Index